Out of the Ashes

The CAFOD/DLT Lent Book 2005

D1321924

Margaret Atkins * **Chris Chivers**
Christopher Jamison * **Patrick Lafon**
Jane Livesey * **Ursula Sharp**

Out of the Ashes

Reflections on the Scripture Readings for Lent 2005

CAFOD
just one world

DARTON · LONGMAN + TODD

First published in Great Britain in 2004 by

CAFOD
Romero Close
Stockwell Road
London SW9 9TY

Darton, Longman and Todd Ltd
1 Spencer Court
140–142 Wandsworth High Street
London SW18 4JJ

© 2004 Margaret Atkins, Chris Chivers, Christopher Jamison,
Patrick Lafon, Jane Livesey and Ursula Sharpe

ISBN 0 232 52581 1

The right of Margaret Atkins, Chris Chivers, Christopher
Jamison, Patrick Lafon, Jane Livesey and Ursula Sharpe to be identified as
authors of this work has been asserted in accordance with the
Copyright, Designs and Patents Act 1988.

Bible quotations are taken predominantly from the New Jerusalem
Bible, published and copyright © 1985 by Darton, Longman and
Todd Ltd and Doubleday, a division of Random House, Inc.

Note: the Hebrew numbering of the Psalms is used. From Psalm 10
to 147 this is ahead of the Greek and Vulgate numbering which is
used in some psalters.

Cover photo: Marcella Haddad. A CAFOD partner organisation in
Brazil provides food and support to Patricia, 11, and her family,
who live in a temporary settlement.
Cover design: Garry Lambert

Text designed and produced by Sandie Boccacci
Set in 9.5/13pt Palatino
Printed and bound in Great Britain
by Cox and Wyman, Reading

Contents

About the authors

Margaret Atkins is a Senior Lecturer in Theology at Trinity and All Saints College, Leeds. She has particular interests in Augustine, Aquinas and ethics, especially environmental ethics.

Chris Chivers, an Anglican priest, is Precentor at Westminster Abbey. He was previously Canon Precentor of St George's Cathedral, Cape Town. He is the author of several books, including *Echoes of a Rainbow Song*, *The Hard Road to Glory* and *The Open Window*, all published in South Africa.

Christopher Jamison OSB is a monk of Worth Abbey in Sussex, where he worked for many years as a teacher, including eight as head teacher. He is now the Abbot of Worth and President of the International Commission on Benedictine Education.

Patrick Lafon is a priest of the Archdiocese of Bamenda. He studied and taught philosophy in Rome before being appointed General Secretary of the Catholic Bishops' Conference of Cameroon.

Jane Livesey CJ is the Provincial Superior of the English Province of the Congregation of Jesus, an apostolic religious order for women, founded by an Englishwoman, Mary Ward, in the early 17th century.

Ursula Sharpe is a Medical Missionary of Mary. She has

worked in Uganda with people with HIV/AIDS and orphans since 1987. She is a nurse and counsellor.

Introduction

'Once again, the Gospel challenges our expectations, exposes the obstacles that we place between ourselves and our deepest happiness.'

As Chris Chivers points out, Lent is never quite what we expect it to be.

The contributors to *Out of the Ashes* each reflect on words that have changed the world. The church's readings during the season of Lent speak of the glory of creation, the preciousness of every human being, each individual known and loved by God, each of us created in God's image and likeness.

For centuries, men and women who had been pushed to the margins by the wealthy and powerful, whose lives had never been considered, whose voices had never been heard, have drawn from the words of the old and new testaments the vision and the strength to claim a different future for themselves and their children.

Each year, we make our own plans to help create this new future, to make the kingdom of God a reality. We decide to give up chocolate biscuits. We make a generous donation to CAFOD or Christian Aid. We join groups campaigning for a change in consumer habits and government policies.

Yet as we place ourselves quietly before God in prayer, and as we search for God in the rough and tumble of service to others, we find a God who is there to welcome us, yet who upsets our rhythm, who knocks us off course.

We begin by thinking Lent is about preaching and we discover it is about learning. We begin by thinking it is about generosity and we discover it is also about our need to be forgiven. We think it is about our need to give and we find it is about our need to receive.

Lent is never what we expect it to be.

BRENDAN WALSH

Out of the Ashes

The CAFOD/DLT Lent Book 2005

Chris Chivers

Ash Wednesday to Saturday after Ash Wednesday

Ash Wednesday

God's *bergies*

Jl 2:12–18; Ps 51; Co 5:20–6:2; Mt 6:1–6, 16–18

> 'As his fellow workers, we beg you once again not to neglect the grace of God that you have received.'
>
> (2 Corinthians 6:1)

It had all started well but then I realised that I'd got things spectacularly wrong. Five hundred office workers had come to the lunchtime Eucharist at the cathedral in Cape Town one Ash Wednesday. I was preaching, stressing the importance of fasting during Lent, when a forlorn-looking group of street people shuffled up the south aisle and wearily sank into their seats. And it suddenly occurred to me how ridiculous it all was. There was I, comfortably off, extolling the virtues of fasting, when the last thing they needed to be told was to fast. They were doing so already. They had no choice. What they needed was some soup and a sandwich.

In a few days' time, the Gospel reading will remind us that we have to know the context in which we're living. We must read the signs of the times, notice what is going on around us. And if we find that hard in everyday life, we can perhaps be forgiven for failing to see the context of today's Gospel passage. It forms part of what we call the Sermon on the Mount, that passage of teaching which begins with the Beatitudes of Jesus. But if Matthew has Jesus talking on the mountain to the in-crowd, to the comfortably off, Luke's Jesus speaks to the down-at-heel, even the destitute, amidst the plains beneath.

Context is everything. It makes sense to tell the comfortably off to fast. It's nonsense, indeed it's blasphemy – as those street people in Cape Town reminded me – to tell the poor to do the same. But those street people also taught me something else. The Afrikaans name by which they are known is *bergie*, literally 'mountain dweller', because centuries ago the indigenous, the poorest Capetonians, lived on the slopes of that city's famous Table Mountain not in the city bowl, on the plains beneath, where the wealthy colonists resided. And that's a good reversal of expectations with which to begin Lent. For it's so often the people who see the spiritual heights, the holy mountain, as their natural inhabitat who need to be confronted by their spiritual poverty and emptiness. Just as it's the poorest of the poor who invariably prove themselves to be the real *bergies*, those who are already God's holy mountain dwellers, if only those of us who lived in the plains could see this.

Thought for the day
If we genuflect before the Blessed Sacrament then we should kneel in the presence of every human being.
(from a sermon of Archbishop Emeritus Desmond Tutu)

Prayer
Lord, help me to see
the reality of your presence,
the challenge of your kingdom,
the gift of your love
in the *bergies* of your holy mountain. Amen.

Taking up the cross: putting on the t-shirt

Dt 30:15–20; Ps 1; Lk 9:22–25

> *'Those who lose his life for my sake will save it.'*
> (Luke 9:24b)

I stand on the steps of the cathedral in Cape Town awaiting Zackie Achmat, the main speaker at a service being held to support the work of the Treatment Action Campaign. TAC's objective is to persuade the South African government to provide anti-retroviral drugs to all those living with HIV and AIDS. In the first instance they have focussed on preventing mother-to-child transmission of HIV. Zackie, who is himself HIV positive, arrives with a thousand TAC supporters and thrusts into my hands the latest campaign t-shirt. He invites me to put it on. I explain that it is difficult for me to do so as I am dressed in cassock and surplice. I will carry the t-shirt instead.

The service begins and, after some readings from different faith communities, Zackie gives the address.

All the while I have been holding my t-shirt. I now look at it, exactly as Zackie is talking about the latest phase of TAC's strategy, which is to encourage as many people as possible simply to wear the very t-shirt I am holding. Emblazoned on the front are the words 'HIV positive'. 'Let us resolve to be united in our humanity. Let each of us wear this t-shirt to show that we will stand against prejudice and with all those who are living with HIV,' says Zackie.

I imagine for a moment what the response might be if I wear the t-shirt to the dinner party I am to attend this evening. All I can see are horrified faces trying to hide behind glasses of Chardonnay and plates of pre-dinner snacks.

I look down at my t-shirt as others, prompted by Zackie's call, are putting on theirs. But faced with the difficulty of fitting the t-shirt over my cassock and surplice, or taking these off in the middle of the cathedral and then putting it on, I hold onto it instead.

'Today I set before you life and death, blessing or curse ... choose life,' says Moses. 'Take up your cross everyday and follow me,' says Jesus. How will we respond? Do we have the courage to put on the t-shirt, and walk to Calvary and beyond?

Thought for the day
We believe in life before death. (Christian Aid slogan)

Prayer
Lord,
give me
the commitment to identify with those living with HIV and AIDS,
the strength to carry with them their cross of pain and suffering,
and the love to realise that this is not a cross of shame,
but your cross of glory.
Amen.

True love

Is 58:1–9; Ps 51; Mt 9:14–15

> *'Is not this the sort of fast that pleases me … to share your bread with the hungry, and shelter the homeless poor?'*
>
> (Isaiah 58:6a, 7)

Ivan, a charmingly cheeky teenager, is one of the many Cape Town street children who've made the cathedral's north porch their home. I see him and his friends often. Most Fridays Ivan invites me to accompany him to the Yizani Day Centre, where he finds food, recreation, and a few hours' rest from the relentlessness of strolling the city's streets. Over a period of months I've made a habit of giving up a couple of hours of my time to go with him to play kerem, a township game like pool, played with cue sticks, on a board with corner pockets and two differently coloured sets of counters. During our early bouts I am hopelessly outclassed. I approach the game like snooker. In true Western style, I concentrate too much on angles and not enough on adventure! And the matches aren't, as a result, much competition – or fun – for Ivan. But as the weeks go on he senses that I could improve, and he becomes my teacher, showing me where and how I must strike the counter to achieve the best results. 'You play good now, Chris,' he says one Friday. The next Friday I use all the skills he's taught me, take my chances and actually win a game off him. And if my smile is broad, Ivan's is broader still.

Our journey through Lent is underway. We've been instructed to fast. And perhaps we've responded by giving up something. But if we've done so, then the prophet Isaiah hits us with some difficult questions about the integrity of what we're doing. We may be fasting, but are we sharing our bread with the hungry, and sheltering the homeless poor? We may have given things up but what have we taken on?

Lenten preachers often contrast the two. But Ivan, my street child friend, has taught me a deeper truth. I gave up some time to be with him and his friends. It was my way, I guess, of responding to Isaiah's call to identify with the poor. But if I gave up my time, he gave up something infinitely more precious since, as one of the most disempowered members of society, he surrendered the only potential hold he had over me – his kerem-playing skills. And in this, he has taught me the true nature of love.

Thought for the day
From what we get, we can make a living; what we give, however, makes a life.

(from *Days of Grace* by Arthur Ashe)

Prayer
Lord,
help me
never to stifle the gifts I see in others,
but to cherish them
as signs of your real presence in the world.
Amen.

A first step

Is 58:9–14; Ps 86:1–6; Lk 5:27–32

> *'You will rebuild the ancient ruins, build up on the old
> foundations. You will be called "breach-mender",
> "Restorer of ruined houses".'*

(Isaiah 58:12)

I am sitting in a civic hall in Guguletu, a Cape Town
township community, in November 1996. A 70-year-old
woman has been called to testify before South Africa's
Truth and Reconciliation Commission concerning the
activities of a policeman in her township. It transpires
that he had come one night with some others and in front
of the woman had shot her son at point-blank range. Two
years later the same officer had returned to arrest her
husband, whom she supposed subsequently to have
been executed. Some time later the policeman came yet
again. This time he took her to a place where he showed
her her husband, still alive. But as her spirits lifted, the
policeman doused the husband with gasoline, set him on
fire and killed him.

As the woman concludes her testimony, the presiding
officer addresses her: 'What would you like the outcome
to be of this hearing?' After a long pause, the woman
answers, 'I would like three things. First, I want to be
taken to the place where my husband was burned, so I
can gather up the dust and give his remains a decent
burial. Second, my son and my husband were my only
family. Therefore, I want this police officer to become my

son, to come twice a month to my home and spend a day with me so I can pour out on him whatever love I still have remaining inside me. Finally, I want this officer to know that I offer him forgiveness because Jesus Christ died to forgive me. Please would someone lead me across the hall so that I can embrace him and let him know that he is truly forgiven.'

As people lead the woman across the room, the police officer, completely overwhelmed, faints. Officials help him, whilst the woman's friends and neighbours, most of them victims of the same sort of violence, begin to sing softly, 'Amazing grace, how sweet the sound, that saved a wretch like me …'

Do we have the courage to take a first step towards forgiveness and reconciliation in our own lives?

Thought for the day

Bid ben bid bont – Whoever would be a leader must be a bridge.

(Armorial motto chosen by George Thomas)

Prayer

Lord,
take my anger,
and make of it an open channel
through which I may see a way forward;
take my pain,
and make of it a well-spring of compassion
for those who have wronged me;
take my suffering,
and make of it a fountain of hope
for the future.
Lord, teach me how to forgive others
as you forgive me. Amen.

Chris Chivers
First Week of Lent

First Sunday of Lent

Roots and branches

Gn 2:7–9, 3:1–7; Ps 51; Ro 5:12–19; Mt 4:1–11

> *'Out of the ground the Lord God made to grow every
> tree that is pleasant to the sight and good for food.'*
> (Genesis 2:9a)

I'll never forget the night that I invited Wilhelm
Verwoerd, grandson of Hendrick Verwoerd, the assassin-
ated architect of apartheid, to preach at the cathedral in
Cape Town. He was clearly daunted by the task. He
sensed an extraordinary irony in a Verwoerd standing in
a pulpit for so long known as the platform for anti-
apartheid opposition. He sensed other tensions too. Just
a few feet behind him lay a memorial to Alfred, Lord
Milner, the very Englishman who had, during the South
African War, sent thousands of Afrikaner women and
children to the first concentration camps the world had
ever known. He was also going to say things about his
journey away from the centre of apartheid philosophy
and belief which his family might find difficult to hear.

But, as he struggled to begin his reflections on the
extraordinary trek he had taken from the heart of the
National Party and its wicked policies of racial segrega-
tion to the heart of the ANC and its hopes for a new
South Africa, he found in the oak trees of his home town
of Stellenbosch – it's also known as Eikestad, literally

'Oak City' – an image that could speak to us all. 'Whilst an oak tree' he said, 'is, on the one hand, firmly rooted in the living soil, quietly growing, slowly fulfilling its unique potential, its branches are, on the other hand, flexible, patiently waiting and waving in the wind.' And that image really hit home for me. Because in my over simplistic view of things, I tended to see the journey Wilhelm and others had walked as an exercise in chopping down trees and starting over again. What he was suggesting was something much more subtle and complex. For though it was tempting to see his Dutch Reformed, Afrikaner roots as rotten to the core, they weren't of course all bad. The fruits they had for so long produced might have been terrible, but branches could be pruned to yield new produce, the roots could be dug around, as Luke suggests in his version of the fig tree parable (Lk 13:6-9), without uprooting the whole tree. And perhaps that's what Lent is in fact about. It would be simple just to chop the whole oak down and start again. Much more challenging to have to live with the tree as it is, prune back some of its branches or dig around it and really get to the root of its transformation.

Thought for the day
We cannot undo the past, but we can and must transcend it. (Mamphela Ramphele, Managing Director, The World Bank)

Prayer
Lord,
give me the grace to know
when I must cut away
the dead branches in my life,
or dig around my roots
to enable their growth and health. Amen.

Sent away, empty handed?

Lv 19:1–2, 11–18; Ps 19; Mt 25:31–46

> *'Go away from me … for I was hungry and you never gave me food.'*
>
> (Matthew 25:41–42)

'Sir, I am from Durban. Have no fear. I am a Zulu. I am a Christian. I've been looking for work. I've just got a job this morning. It starts tomorrow. But I have a wife and four children. Sir, I need money to feed them today. Please can you help me?'

The crisply rehearsed phrases of this Zulu man confront me wherever I meet him in Cape Town over a two-year period. Sometimes the number of children changes but the request is always the same. He never remembers that I've heard his speech so many times before. He must be lying. I don't give him a cent. Sometimes I don't even bother to direct him to the cathedral's Soup Bowl because I find him extremely tiresome.

My response to him is greatly hampered by my suspicion that he isn't telling the truth. Clearly he's not rich but he doesn't seem destitute either. So I can send him away empty-handed and not feel too much of a conscience. But each time I meet him there's a nagging feeling at the back of my mind. What if one day he were to be very much in need? I wouldn't be able to tell because his seeming untruthfulness has destroyed any potential trust I might have in what he says. But what chance do the poor have to establish such trust?

Several years on, those thoughts prey on my conscience, for the kingdom belongs, so Jesus tells us in today's Gospel, to those who feed the hungry, welcome the stranger, and clothe the naked. And – which is the bit most of us who are comfortably off tend to avoid – it is to be taken away from those who don't.

The context for me has changed. I'm now in London not Cape Town, but the pleading is still the same as I walk down Victoria Street from Westminster Abbey.

'Father, I'm from Manchester. Don't be afraid. I won't hurt you. I'm a Christian. I've been looking for work. I've just got a job this morning. It starts tomorrow. But I have a wife and children. Father, I need money to feed them today. Please can you help me?'

I never give money. If I'm honest, the apparent dishonesty of the requests still irritates me. I do give food, but I still feel guilty. And though I attempt to resolve that feeling by saying to myself that it's structures at a national and international level that need to be changed, those words of Jesus haunt me: 'In so far as you neglected to do this to one of the least of these, you neglected to do it to me.'

Thought for the day

Give all thou canst; high Heaven rejects the lore of nicely-calculated less or more.

(from 'Within King's College Chapel, Cambridge', William Wordsworth)

Prayer

Lord,
help me to bridge the gap between
truth and falsehood,
to build real trust
through the riskiness of your love and compassion.
Amen.

You can't stop at evil

Is 55:10–11; Ps 34; Mt 6:7–15

> *'Do not put us to the test, but save us from the evil one.'*
>
> (Matthew 6:13

Pain, conquered. Suffering, transcended. The narratives of contemporary South Africa cry out for the world's attention. And none more so than that of Father Michael Lapsley. Cruelly maimed by a letter bomb, which blew off both his hands and caused him to lose an eye, his subsequent – and relentless – pursuit of healing and reconciliation for all the suffering of the world is truly remarkable. He could, like so many, have been filled with hatred and bitterness. But to see him celebrate the Eucharist, and to hold up his metal prosthetic limbs, is to know the presence of the risen Christ who bears the scars of human sin and evil but is not shackled by them. But most remarkable of all is the way in which his journey from death to new life began even as he was being wheeled on a hospital trolley for emergency surgery, moments after he had opened the letter bomb.

The doctors couldn't give him any painkillers. They had to keep him conscious until he was sedated for surgery. So Michael's friends surrounded him, trying to comfort him. They had to shout because both his eardrums had been shattered in the explosion. But Michael clearly knew who they were, since he began to cry out to one of them, 'Pray with me, Phyllis.'

Phyllis was taken aback. She didn't know where to start. So Michael asked her to say the Lord's Prayer. She struggled to remember ... 'and deliver us from evil. Amen.' But Michael immediately said, 'Go on.' 'That's where it ends,' came the reply. 'You can't stop there,' said Michael. 'You can't stop at evil ... for thine is the kingdom, the power and ... the glory.'

The story isn't meant to end with evil. But, so often, that's where it seems to stop. We suffer at the hands of others, or because of our own folly. We are victims. Sometimes we go one stage better. We make it through. We are survivors. Yet the Gospel uses not just the language of survival. It promises victory. But for sin and evil to be defeated a first step must be taken. And in Matthew's version of the Lord's Prayer this comes through the costly business of letting go – his emphasis on forgiveness (Mt 6:14). For when we let go of our hurt and pain, when we refuse to let them dictate our lives, then we begin the journey to liberation and wholeness.

Thought for the day
To forgive is not just to be altruistic; it is the best form of self interest.

(Archbishop Emeritus Desmond Tutu)

Prayer
Lord,
help me to take the first step
towards wholeness and holiness,
by forgiving the sins of those who have wronged me,
even as I seek forgiveness for my wrongdoing.
Amen.

A ripple of self-knowledge and hope

Jon 3:1–10; Ps 51; Lk 11:29–32

> *'God saw their efforts to renounce their evil behaviour.'*
> (Jonah 3:10b)

We live in an age of the grand apology. Political leaders everywhere seem to be saying 'Sorry' for the sins of their forbears. An American President, for the evils of the slave trade. A New Zealand Prime Minister, for oppression of the Maoris. Even British politicians, from time to time, appear to express regret for the sins of colonialism. It's easy to be cynical about such apologies. But there is, I think, a genuine acknowledgement that we inhabit a history which has consequences.

Someone, somewhere along the line, has to own up to the impact of all that, to stick their head over the parapet and take responsibility. And, it seems, rather a lot of people are giving this a go. One Remembrance Sunday, at the cathedral in Cape Town, I attempt to join them.

A few days earlier I am preparing my sermon sitting quietly in my stall when a young man comes in and asks me what I am up to. So I share with him the images I am using as props for my reflections. One is a photograph of the concentration camps the British set up nearby for Afrikaner women and children during the South African War. The other, a painting of Job Maseko, a black South African who sank a ship at Tobruk during the Second World War with a home-made bomb he fashioned whilst a prisoner of war. I explain that I am trying to correct the almost overwhelmingly white, British images with which I usually fill the two minutes' silence. As we talk he helps me to realise that what I am really trying to do is to overcome my racism.

So, in my sermon, I share something of this with the congregation. And boy, do I get some comeback from what I say! 'You've just confirmed what we always thought of the British … all racists', remarks one person. But when it comes to the time for me to leave the cathedral the same person now thanks me for what I'd said all those months before. 'I didn't know it at the time, but you helped me to overcome my racism too.'

Taking responsibility – especially for the actions of others – can be a costly and somewhat ambiguous business. But it seems to be the divine way of doing things. God saw their efforts to renounce their evil behaviour, and he relented … he sent his only begotten Son to walk with and for them the ambiguous but life-changing road to the cross.

Thought for the day
Each time a person stands up for an ideal, or acts to improve the lot of others, or strikes out against injustice, they send forth a tiny ripple of hope.
(adapted from an address to students at the University of Cape Town, 1966, by Robert F Kennedy)

Prayer
Lord,
give me the courage
to own and own up to
the history of which I am a part
so that I may begin to transcend its worst features.
Amen.

Reclaiming human dignity

Est 4:1–3, 5:12–14; Ps 138; Mt 7:7–12

'Ask and it will be given to you.'

(Matthew 7:7)

One Thursday morning I am sitting in my office at the cathedral in Cape Town when I receive a phone call from Amelia Poswa. Amelia runs an informal children's home in Mfeleni, a tiny township community on the outskirts of the city. She looks after 80 youngsters amongst whom are orphans, many children living with HIV, and survivors of abuse or rape. There has been terrible flooding in the large township nearby. She has been overwhelmed with additional children who need clothing, food and shelter. There are now about 140 children in her tiny home. This is a real emergency. Can I help?

I ring Mary my wife, who bundles our two sons into the back of the car and collects me. We head off to Mfeleni and buy some essentials en route.

We arrive and make a plan to assist Amelia over the next few weeks, whilst our toddler sons, Dominic and Gregory, play with a group of children much the same age. As they do so, I notice that Dominic has taken a particular shine to the only visible toy in the yard in front of the house. It is a little plastic motorbike.

When the time comes for us to go I know that we will have trouble wresting the bike from Dominic – whose favourite phrase at the moment is that most characteristically Western, 'Mine'. I gently – but purposefully –

explain to him that it isn't his bike. I cajole him. Give him the five minute warning about its return. I do all the things that those parenting books tell you you must do. But can I get him to give it back? No. In the end I have to take it from him, as he throws a tantrum and wails his lungs out.

Swiftly returning him to the car I feel terribly embarrassed that our eldest son's behaviour has so graphically brought home to me the obvious contrast between the immense privileges he enjoys and the abject poverty of Amelia's children. But then I notice that the group of two and three-year-old children, with whom Dominic has been playing, is busy having what looks like a conference. And a few seconds later I watch – absolutely speechless – as one child is deputed by the group to bring the bike to Dominic and to give it to him.

It's a kingdom moment I'll never forget. For, whilst the structural inequalities of the world lock those children into a power dynamic which forces them to survive on hand-outs, they now turn this hierarchy on its head. As they do so they assert their innate human dignity and help me to reclaim my own.

Thought for the day
Give freely that others may be free to give.

(Life Style Movement slogan)

Prayer
Lord,
make of my life a gift and blessing for others,
so that as I see with your compassion,
and respond with your love,
I may release in them the riches of your transforming
grace. Amen.

19

Saying sorry

Ez 18:21–28; Ps 130; Mt 5:20—26

> *'First go and be reconciled with your brother or sister.'*
> (Matthew 5:24b)

I am sitting in the Good Hope Centre in Cape Town one Wednesday late in August 1996. There is a great sense of anticipation amongst those around me since F W de Klerk is to table a submission from the New National Party before the Truth and Reconciliation Commission. Everyone is wondering what he will say. Will he apologise for the sins of apartheid? 'The Nats messed up my whole life,' the person next to me remarks. 'I wanted to be here so that I could tell my grandchildren that I was in the room when they explained their apartheid policy.' They may do that, I think to myself, but will they apologise?

The submission is heard in absolute silence, as de Klerk explains the apartheid years which he, in part, presided over and helped to dismantle. The tension in the air – the prelude to his anticipated apology – is palpable. And then come the words we have all been waiting to hear. 'I apologise for all the sufferings caused ... '

But as the words sink in, a momentary release of tension gives rise to a surge of anger and outrage. For though de Klerk apologises for the evil consequences of state-sanctioned racism, he doesn't actually say 'Sorry' for the policy itself. The line he takes is that the objectives

20

of a system which divided people on the basis of their skin colour were right. It just didn't work out in practise.

'Sorry' is perhaps one of the most over-used of words. And too often it's used as a kind of bargaining counter, a final card to play in the game of life. If all else fails, say 'Sorry' and we'll somehow con our way through, and get our own way. But we all know when an apology is genuine and what a difference it can make. For when it's heartfelt, when we know the person saying 'Sorry' has not only owned up to and owned the consequences of their actions but also the motivation behind them, then their 'Sorry' liberates them and us. 'Ah well, I'm kind of Sorry …' – de Klerk's sort of Sorry – sadly compounds the problem. Since its failure to take responsibility actually perpetuates the oppression of those who most need to be liberated. What is required instead is human transaction at a much deeper level, transaction that actually enables real reconciliation across and between communities. So, how are we going to get that started today? To whom must we say 'Sorry', so that we can meaningfully go to the altar with our gift and share it with others?

Thought for the day
It's the tiny drops of water that wear away the stone.
(favourite African proverb of Njongonkulu Ndungane,
Archbishop of Cape Town)

Prayer
Lord, when I say sorry,
help me to mean it.
Amen.

Lenten laughter

Dt 26:16–19; Ps 119:1–8; Mt 5:43–48

'Love your enemies'

(Matthew 5: 45a)

Clergy are not renowned for their one-liners. But in response to a parishioner's enquiry a clergy friend of mine excelled himself. 'Why', he was asked, 'has that terrible new Canon Precentor invited an imam to preach at the cathedral on Sunday?'

'I shouldn't worry, my dear,' came the disarmingly amusing reply, 'he's invited a Jewish drag queen the next week!'

And indeed I had. For as part of a Lenten series I'd asked South Africa's leading satirist, Pieter-Dirk Uys – better known as the character Evita Bezuidenhout – to address the subject of 'Laughter as an agent of transformation'. He gave his sermon the title: 'No-one died laughing'. 'Should I come as Evita or Pieter?' he asked. We played safe. He came as himself.

He began by pointing to the clergy. 'What a change it is to be in a place where other people are wearing the dresses.' Next he pointed to himself. 'As a Jew and an Afrikaner, I belong to both the chosen people.' And he continued in a deceptively light-hearted vein which masked the seriousness of what he was saying. We roared with laughter, for instance, when he thanked the apartheid government for giving him all his material. And we continued to do so as he reminded us of Helen

Suzman's annual question in parliament: 'How many people this year have had their racial classification changed?' The answer, direct from Hansard, brought the house down. 'Five coloureds have become whites. Two whites have become coloureds. One Chinese has become white. Two blacks have become coloureds. One white has become black ...' It was absolutely ridiculous. But it was all of course frighteningly true.

Love your enemies, Jesus demands of us in today's Gospel. And one way of doing that is to laugh at them because this wrong foots them. But what we laugh at in others is invariably what we most fear in ourselves. So laughter has a two-edged quality. It's important that this is so because we shan't be able to love the enemies out there unless we've got to grips with what's going on in here, with the demons within us. We start confronting them, not by laughing them off, but by laughing at them, for this exposes just how ridiculous they are.

And by this stage in Lent we all need a dose of such laughter to prick our bubble of piety. For laughter of course is so close to love, love which can conquer the enemies both within and without.

Thought for the day
The human race has one really effective weapon, and that is laughter. (Mark Twain)

Prayer
Lord,
give me the grace
to laugh at my own foolishness,
and to see through it the love
that draws me closer to my neighbour and to you.
Amen.

Margaret Atkins

Second Week of Lent

Second Sunday of Lent

The father of three nations

Gn 12:1–4a; Ps 33; 2 Tim 1:8–10; Mt 17:1–9

> *'And I will make of you a great nation, and I will bless
> you, and make your name great, so that you will be a
> blessing.'*
>
> (Genesis 12:3)

We begin the week with Abraham being called to be the
father of a new nation. In fact, he has become the father
of not one, but three, of the great faiths of the world:
Judaism, Christianity and Islam. Perhaps, then, it is a
good opportunity to reflect upon what is shared by the
three 'peoples of the Book' descended from Abraham. At
this time in particular we might think of the three funda-
mental practices of Lent, prayer, fasting and almsgiving,
and of the repentance which they express. Lent,
Ramadan and Yom Kippur are often seen as signs of dis-
tinctiveness, marking out the worshippers of one faith
from those of another. Yet it is precisely by living our
own faith as well as we are able, by committing ourselves
seriously during Lent to the disciplines of prayer, fasting
and almsgiving, that we come closer to those who think
differently about God.

The readings begin with what we share with other
believers, and move on to what is distinctive. The story

of the transfiguration gives us a preview of the resurrection, as it were, reminding us of where our Lenten journey will end. It also makes uncompromising claims about Jesus himself. He is the successor to Moses, the bringer of the Law, and to Elijah, the greatest of the prophets. Jesus' shining face recalls Moses' own when he spoke to God on Mount Sinai; the bright cloud represents the glory of the presence of God. Moses and Elijah are there, yet it is Jesus alone who is described by the voice of God as God's beloved Son.

We share much in our monotheism and in our religious practices with our Jewish and Muslim brothers and sisters. Yet we differ from them, in a way that shocks them, in our identification of Jesus as the Son of God. The Christian claims are paradoxical in identifying a limited human being with the revelation of the limitless God. They are more paradoxical still in a second way: as Jesus comes down the mountain, he warns his disciples that the Son of Man will suffer and die.

Thought for the day
True peace and understanding among the faiths can only be based on absolute honesty, neither neglecting what is shared nor obscuring what is distinctive.

Prayer
God of Abraham,
bring peace and mutual understanding among Jews, Christians and Muslims.
May Christians be inspired by the revelation of God in Christ as one who repays suffering with forgiveness, and in his name work tirelessly for reconciliation.
Amen

Second Monday of Lent

Hearts of flesh

Dn 9:4–10; Ps 79; Lk 6:36–38

> *Be compassionate as your Father is compassionate.*
>
> (Luke 6:36)

Yesterday, we encountered Jesus as the Son of Man transfigured on the mountain, immediately before he predicted his own death and suffering. The readings of this week repeatedly overturn our human expectations in this way. In doing so, they identify the obstacles that prevent us from coming closer to God, those obstacles which we hope to dislodge through the disciplines of Lent. In Luke's Gospel today Jesus calls his disciples to imitate the Father by being merciful or compassionate. Matthew reports a similar phrase in the Sermon on the Mount, 'Be perfect as your heavenly Father is perfect.' Perhaps Jesus said each of these things at different times, or perhaps Matthew and Luke is each in his own way interpreting the same saying. In either case, it seems that to be perfect, as Christians understand it, means in particular to be compassionate. The obstacle to perfection, then, is that hardness of heart so vividly evoked by the words of the Lord to the prophet Ezekiel, 'I will take out of your flesh the heart of stone and give you a heart of flesh.'

Again, the Gospel reverses merely human expectations. We can see this from today's Psalm. Our liturgy gives us a carefully edited version, including the prayers for God's mercy, but omitting the verses in which the Psalmist cries for vengeance on his enemies: 'Pour out your anger on the nations that do not know you,' 'Let the avenging of the outpoured blood of your servants be known among the nations before our eyes.' The Psalms, in all their unbridled honesty, capture the ordinary human emotions of resentment and thirst for revenge.

The Gospel asks for something different: do not judge, do not condemn, be ready to pardon. In other words, exercise our extraordinary God-given capacity to imagine ourselves in the shoes of others. It is through that imaginative sympathy that we human beings, alone of the animals, learn to seek for justice. But grace can lift us beyond even the sense of justice, which so often tempts us to revenge, and call us instead to mercy and compassion.

Thought for the day
Vengeance is human; it is mercy that is divine.

Prayer
Lord,
through our Lenten discipline, teach us compassion.
Where we have hearts of stone, give us hearts of flesh,
so that we may be inspired to forgive those who have
hurt us,
and to give generously to those in need.
Amen.

Wisdom or arrogance?

Is 1:10, 16–20; Ps 51; Mt 23:1–12

You have only one teacher, the Christ.

(Matthew 23:10)

Wisdom, we are told, is a gift of the Holy Spirit; mere knowledge, on the other hand, can be an obstacle between us and God. For cleverness and learning can make us proud, when we imagine that they come from ourselves, and forget that they have been given. They can also make us arrogant, when we use them to make other people follow our bidding. 'Knowledge is power': that might be the slogan of the so-called 'knowledge economy'. Once again, Jesus overturns normal assumptions: 'The greatest among you must be your servant. Anyone who exalts himself will be humbled, and anyone who humbles himself will be exalted.'

'Do not be called teacher.' That saying is perhaps even harder to swallow. St Augustine wrote a whole book called *The Teacher* precisely to explain it, arguing that Christ is our only teacher because all our understanding comes from him. St Thomas Aquinas wryly pointed out that even Augustine was happy to call other people 'teacher' elsewhere in his writings.

Perhaps, then, we cannot follow the letter of this command. But we can follow it in spirit, if we remember that all our networks of communications, all our theories and our technologies, all the systems we create and the books that we write are not, ultimately, our own. They have been given to us, and are worth nothing, and worse than nothing, unless we offer them back to their Giver.

How are we to do that? The answer is not to be found in libraries or databanks, but in the simple words of the prophet: 'Cease to do evil. Learn to do good, search for justice, help the oppressed, be just to the orphan, plead for the widow.' It is as straightforward as that. Here, then, is a test by which to judge all our education and all our inventions in this 'age of technology'. Do we design them and use them for justice, with an eye on the poor? Or are they just tools for our own advancement, to make us, the rich, still richer, to keep the powerful firmly entrenched in their power?

Thought for the day

It is not what you know, but how you use it, that matters.

Prayer

Christ, our only teacher,
give us the wisdom to use all our knowledge, our intelligence and our inventiveness
for your purposes,
to seek justice,
to help the oppressed,
to defend those who need our protection.
Amen

The need for self-knowledge

Jer 18:18-20; Ps 31; Mt 20:17-28

> *You do not know what you are asking.*
>
> (Matthew 20:22)

The Psalmist and Jeremiah are all too aware of the hostility that a just person can inspire; they describe themselves, with a degree of self-pity, as victims of their enemies' intrigues. Jesus makes a similar point about himself, but in a manner far more detached, describing his future fate almost as if he is talking of somebody else: 'They will condemn him to death and will hand him over to the pagans to be mocked and scourged and crucified.'

With delicious irony, Matthew links this passage directly to the request of the mother of James and John for her sons to be granted a place of honour. What fools we make ourselves look with our ambitions for ourselves and our children! At the very point when Jesus is predicting for himself the most degrading death of all, a pushy mother comes along and asks for her sons to bask in his reflected glory. Again, Jesus patiently teaches the lesson that our ordinary expectations are overturned by the values of the Kingdom: 'Anyone who wants to be great among you must be your servant, and anyone who wants to be first among you must be your slave.'

It is only very rarely that anyone in the Gospels tries to tell Jesus what to do; when they do, they often receive an implicit rebuke that opens their eyes to a truth bigger than they have imagined. Think, for example, of Peter's protest against a similar prediction of Jesus' suffering, met with the hard response, 'Get behind me Satan!'; or of Martha's demand to tell her sister to help her, to which Jesus replies, 'Mary has chosen the better part.' Here again Jesus insists on unsettling the cosy illusions: 'You do not know what you are asking.' Even when they protest that they can drink the cup that he must drink, we are left unconvinced: for did not all the disciples abandon him when he was arrested? Underlying their competitiveness, underlying their fearfulness, lurks a lack of self-knowledge. They must learn, then, to recognise their weakness before they can be given strength.

Thought for the day
What illusions are we giving up for Lent?

Prayer
Lord,
help us through the prayer and penance of Lent
to free ourselves from illusions about ourselves
and about the goals that are worth striving for.
In this way, may we come,
through greater self-knowledge,
to a greater knowledge of you.
Amen.

God and Mammon

Jer 17:5–10; Ps 1; Lk 16:19–31

> *A blessing on the man who puts his trust in the Lord.*
> (Jeremiah 17:7)

Most of us, like Dives, possess far more than we need. Most of us, like Dives, from time to time encounter real poverty, whether in person or on the screens of our televisions. Most of us, like Dives, have sometimes kept a tight hold on our purse-strings. So what prompts us to respond like this? As Jeremiah bluntly puts it:

> The heart is more devious than any other thing,
> perverse too; who can pierce its secrets?

Jeremiah's answer to his own question is, of course, the Lord who searches the heart. And in Luke's Gospel Jesus is portrayed as a master of human psychology, telling a story full of hints about the particular deviousness of Dives' heart. We learn of the love of luxury that persuades him that he needs all his money for himself, to keep himself supplied with fashionable clothing and haute cuisine. We learn of the hardness of heart that prevents him from offering even the left-over crusts to Lazarus, although, as we later discover, he actually knows him by name. We learn of his religious error in failing to trust what the Scriptures say about the afterlife – he is portrayed, it seems, as a follower of the Sadducees, who did not believe in life after death. And we learn of his arrogance, such that even after he has discovered the truth, he still wants to treat Lazarus as an errand-boy, to be sent off at his pleasure to warn his brothers.

There are two questions here: why did Dives love his riches so much? And why did Dives love Lazarus so little? We might find the answer by contrasting the frantic and competitive consumerism of our own society with Jeremiah's portrait of the man who puts his hope in the Lord: 'He is like a tree by the waterside that thrusts its roots to the stream; when the heat comes it feels no alarm, its foliage stays green.' Underlying our anxious search for status and security is a collective failure to trust in God. That is why we need to be so wealthy, and why sometimes we cannot afford to be kind.

Thought for the day
The more complicated our lives, the harder we will find it to notice when others are in need.

Prayer
Lord God,
restore to us through prayer our trust in you,
teach us through fasting our solidarity with those in need,
and liberate us through the giving of alms from an undue attachment to wealth.
Amen.

Fear of dreams

Gn 37:3–4, 12–13, 17–28; Ps 105; Mt 21:33–43, 45–46

Then we shall see what becomes of his dreams.

(Genesis 37:20)

Joseph was not the most tactful of people. It is hard not to sympathise with his brothers when you remember the way that he blurted out to them his dreams about their wheat-sheaves bowing to his, and the sun, moon and stars bowing to himself. As annoying little brothers go, this one took some beating. But Joseph had more to him than mere tactlessness; you might even say that his lack of tact was a by-product of his virtues - the fearlessness that enabled him to speak the truth, the integrity that made him resist Potiphar's wife, the energy, determination and sheer competence with which he did everything entrusted to him, so that even in prison he was a leader of men.

Joseph was both a dreamer and a man of action. Indeed, it is precisely because he took dreams so seriously, both his own and those of others, that he was so effective in whatever he did. His brothers make an interesting contrast here, indecisive in their good and their bad intentions alike. First they plan to kill him. Reuben is against the plot, but has not got the courage to speak out openly. It looks as if Judah is uneasy about it too, so he thinks up the idea of selling Joseph to the Ishmaelites, and his brothers readily fall in with the change of plan. One suspects that if Reuben had refused straightaway to let them kill Joseph, they might all have simply backed down. As it is, he is too weak even to resist their cowardly deception of their poor father, Jacob, whom they fool into thinking that Joseph is dead, simply to cover their own backs.

There was more to the brothers' rejection of Joseph than mere jealously. They feared his strength of character because they themselves were weak. They scoffed at his dreams because they had none of their own. Cynicism is the coward's response to the problems of the world, for the cynic pretends that nothing can be done to relieve them. It takes a dreamer to make a real difference.

Thought for the day
It is not the cynics, but the dreamers, who can change the world.

Prayer
Teach us, Lord,
to respond to the problems of poverty and injustice
with energy, imagination and decisiveness.
Give us the courage to dream dreams,
and the skill and determination
to turn them into reality.
Amen.

The joy of youth

Mi 7:14–15, 18–20; Ps 103:1–4, 9–12; Lk 15:1–3, 11–32

So that your youth is renewed like the eagle's.
(Psalm 103:5)

It is usually worth checking which bits have been missed out of the Responsorial Psalm, since it is not always those blood-curling curses upon the Psalmist's enemies. Today, for example, one of the most beautiful verses in the Old Testament has been omitted from Psalm 103: 'who satisfies you with good as long as you live, so that your youth is renewed like the eagle's'.

We associate youthfulness with joy, symbolised by the energy and freedom of a soaring eagle. Yet the younger generation in our parable is notably lacking in *joie de vivre*. The one son has sought his happiness in temporary stimulation, as so many of our own youngsters seek it in sex and drugs and drink. Like many of them, he is left weary and depressed. His elder brother has sought his in a grim devotion to duty, again like so many of our own youngsters, tied as they are to the demands of jobs and qualifications and debts, often to finance their very entertainments. Like many of them, he is tired and resentful. It is only the father who understands how to celebrate.

It is the father whose youth has been renewed like the eagle's. For he knows that neither pleasure nor duty should be treated as goals in themselves, since pleasure will quickly dissolve into dissipation, and duty harden into resentment. He is driven instead by a deep-seated love: the Greek word translated as 'he had compassion' means literally 'he felt it in his guts'. His generosity and forgiveness breaks the cycle of despair, restoring his younger son to hope and self-respect. And to his elder son too, he offers the opportunity to see life afresh, to rediscover what music and dancing can mean.

Once again, the Gospel challenges our expectations, to expose the obstacles that we place between ourselves and our deepest happiness. The elder son knew how to work, the younger son knew how to play, but neither could recognise the goodness that would satisfy them. Only the father, out of the depth of his compassion, knew how to find, and how to generate, joy.

Thought for the day
The purpose of Lent is renewing our youth.

Prayer
Loving Father,
when we are distracted by the temptations of pleasure,
or embittered by the pressures of work,
help us to turn to you.
May we be renewed through your compassion,
and learn to celebrate joyfully with others
the good things that give true satisfaction.
Amen.

Christopher Jamison

Third week of Lent

Third Sunday of Lent

Living water

Ex 17:3–7; Ps 95; Rom 5:1–2, 5–8; Jn 4:5–42

> *Jesus said to her, 'Give me a drink'.*
>
> (John 4.8)

Those of us lucky enough to have visited the Holy Land know how much we need to keep water to hand in order to survive the heat. How much more is this true for the people who live in Israel-Palestine? In this unreconciled part of the world, politics is often the politics of water. Each side tries to ensure it has access to a well or seeks to direct a water course towards its settlement or town. People are fighting for water, so that the wadi and the well are as significant now as in biblical times.

The Exodus story of the people of Israel wandering in the desert 'tormented by thirst' is true today of both Israelis and Palestinians. As both sides struggle for control of the West Bank, they struggle for access to water. For the Palestinians in particular, the wadis and the wells are sources of justice as well as of water.

The need for water, the enmity of Jews and Samaritans, the oppression of women, all these come together in the remarkable gospel story of the encounter at the well between Jesus and the Samaritan woman.

She is shocked not only to be addressed by Jesus but

above all to be asked to help him. This request quickly leads to an offer: the offer of 'living water'. The woman's reply is marvellously practical: 'You have no bucket, Sir'. This is typical of our response to the preaching of Jesus; it is the modern equivalent of 'Come off it, get real'. Step by step, Jesus leads the woman to appreciate that he is serious, that the offer is real. The water he offers will come not from Jacob's deep well but from an even deeper source, 'a spring inside' and this interior spring will provide water 'welling up to eternal life'.

When we face difficulties, we quickly forget that the source of life is 'a spring inside', inside me and inside the other people involved, even my enemies. In this third week of Lent, I invite you to focus on 'a spring inside'.

Thought for the day

If today is a day of rest for you, take time to rejoice 'because the love of God has been poured into our hearts by the Holy Spirit which has been given us', as the second reading at Mass reminded us.

Prayer

Oh God of Abraham, our father in faith,

hear the prayers of faithful Jews, Christians and Muslims everywhere.

The spring which you have planted in the heart of all people needs constantly refreshing.

Refresh, we pray, the sources of peace inside all who live in the Holy Land.

Through Jesus Christ, refresh the spring in my heart today

so that it may well up to eternal life, where he is Lord for ever and ever.

Amen.

The God of simplicity

2 Kings 5:1–15; Ps 42–43; Lk 4:24–30

> *When they heard this all the synagogue were filled with rage.*
>
> (Luke 4:28)

Following on from Sunday's readings, water continues as a theme throughout this week. Namaan the Syrian is healed by the water of the Jordan. He is an important man, wealthy and powerful, and he cannot believe that healing his leprosy will be as simple as washing in the Jordan. He expects special potions or sophisticated techniques, but instead he is led to a comparatively small river for a wash. To this day, visitors to the Jordan are surprised by the river's small scale compared to the other famous rivers of the world. Yet this humble river has been the channel of God's strength and grace on many occasions. So Namaan finally accepts that this poor river in this poor land is the source of health for him, and God heals him.

In the preaching of Jesus in the synagogue at Nazareth, a similarly unlikely offer is made, namely that the son of Joseph, a local carpenter, is the fulfilment of people's hopes and desires. This offer is rejected in his own land because the familiar and the simple do not fit people's understanding of the places where God works.

The God we make for ourselves works in technicolour and with special effects. Some of our worship styles can foster this image. Yet time and again the prophets say that God is not in the spectacular but in the gentle breeze, in the simple water and in the humble person. Jesus places himself firmly in that prophetic tradition and is not surprised when his hearers find his teaching as difficult to accept as those of Elijah and Elisha, the greatest of the prophets.

Loving the familiar partner, being patient with our children, having time for those who offer us their simple work: here is where God is speaking to us. In these places, God calls us not to passivity but to action, action to meet the rights and the needs of the ordinary people around us. Communion with those among whom we live may be more difficult than generosity towards the stranger who we only meet in a CAFOD poster.

Thought for the day
Today, be open to finding a healing word or a gracious action from a simple and unexpected source.

Prayer
Lord,

help us to be open to your presence where we least expect it.

You are so different to humans that you can restore human life in ways that we would never consider.

Thank you for your presence which is both beyond us and close to us.

Thank you for your love which is so simple and so great.

Amen.

The blame culture

Dn 3:25, 34–43; Ps 25; Mt 18:21–35

> *'How often should I forgive? ...' Jesus replied, 'Not seven times but seventy-seven times.'*
>
> (Matthew 18:21–22)

A phrase from the Lord's Prayer sums up to today's Gospel: 'Forgive us our trespasses as we forgive those who trespass against us.' Yet we are not always conscious of just how many people we consider to have trespassed against us. Consider for a moment how much we blame other people and indeed ourselves. Typically, we blame other people for problems at work: a colleague is impossible to work with, a boss does not listen. Some of us attach blame to our family: a parent neglected me, a sibling dominated me. More generally, we blame structures: the government, the economy. More profoundly, we blame ourselves for things that are not our fault, such as the illness of a family member.

Now some of this blaming may be justified but our problem is that we live in a blame culture. If something goes wrong, somebody must always be to blame. This is seen in the increasing readiness to sue people; there are no longer genuine accidents, somebody must always be responsible, somebody must always be blamed.

Underlying this is a growing refusal to accept that life is precarious and fragile. Those of us who live in rich communities are steeped in this culture of ease. This underlying attitude considers an easy life to be a right and any difficulty to be a mistake for which somebody must be responsible. In such an atmosphere, forgiveness and humility do not come easily. People see humility as weakness and forgiveness as a failure to stand up for our rights.

The prophet Daniel assumes that his suffering is due to lack of faith among the people of Israel; he repents, offers a humble prayer and asks for God to treat them gently. Our difficulties are our responsibility, he insists, but because God is gentle and merciful, he can lead us through them by his wonderful deeds.

Thought for the day
Notice how much blaming happens around you and in your thoughts, including how much you blame yourself.

Prayer
Gentle Lord,
give me the faith to accept this precarious life as your gift so that I may live joyfully.
Set me free from blaming others
so that I might be forgiving towards them.
Help me to take responsibility for my life
but not to blame myself.
Treat us gently, as you yourself are gentle.
Let your name win glory, Lord.
Amen.

The fullness of love

Dt 4:1, 5–9; Ps 147; Mt 5:17–19

'I have come not to abolish but to fulfil.'
(Matthew 5:17)

This week's readings began with the theme of water and then moved on to forgiveness. What brings these two themes together is baptism, because Lent is the Christian community's special time for preparing adults who wish to be baptised. In this third week of Lenten preparation, the catechumens (those being instructed for baptism) are invited to a deeper understanding of Christian faith. At a special liturgy during the week, they listen to a recitation of the Creed which the celebrant introduces saying, 'The words are few but the mysteries they contain are great.'

So today's readings are part of the awesome project of introducing people to the depths of the faith, just as Moses invites his hearers to appreciate the depths of the laws and customs of Israel. The purpose of the Law of Moses is to enable us to love God and our neighbour. Jesus wants to take this process even further, not by abolishing the Law but by completing it. So for Jesus loving our neighbour involves not only avoiding murder but also turning the other cheek. Jesus completes the Law by showing us the fullness of love in his teaching and in his life, especially in his death where he truly turned the other cheek and loved his enemies.

'If you are to be true partners with God in the transfiguration of his world … you must begin by understanding that as much as God loves you, God equally loves your enemies' (Desmond Tutu). In the Creed, 'We acknowledge one baptism for the forgiveness of sins' – everybody's sins, not just mine. The one who is 'Light from Light' wants to become incarnate in you and in all people.

In the developed economies of the world we live with a lot of artificial light, a sign of 'power' in every sense of the word. This artificial power and light can blind us to the fact that we are in need of a change of heart to live out the Creed. Today, as every day, the process of conversion begins anew with me.

Thought for the day
Identify with those who are preparing for baptism this Easter and see how the Creed invites you to love as Christ loved.

Prayer
Lord Jesus Christ,
I believe that you are true God from true God.
May I allow you to become real in my life
so that the Word becomes flesh again.
Amen.

The humiliation of the comfortable

Jr 7:23–28; Ps 95; Lk 11:14–23

> *'When a strong man, fully armed, guards his castle,*
> *his property is safe.'*
>
> (Luke 11:22)

My monastic community has worked in Peru for many years and once, when I was visiting, I travelled the main highway from Lima towards the Andes. I was being driven by a friend and we became caught in a long queue of traffic at a major junction in a town. Suddenly, amidst the typically chaotic roadside of urban Peru, there stood a completely naked young man. People went about their business, policemen directed the traffic and nobody took any notice of him. The young man slowly scavenged among the rubbish, picked up plastic bags and occasionally put something in his mouth. I instinctively wanted to get out of the car and give him something to clothe his humiliating nakedness. I blurted out something to my friend, who replied that Yes, well, he's probably a poor *loco* (madman). The traffic moved on and we with it, but the image has haunted me ever since.

The young man stood like a prophet among the people; exposed and crazy, with nobody paying him any attention. The distressing question is, how could you pay attention, unless you changed your whole plan for the day, interrupted your business and redirected all your energy to caring for him? Even then, he might not co-operate and then you would look a complete fool.

We just don't listen to prophets; we *can't* listen, because if we actually heard what they said, everything in our lives would have to change. Some people are called by God to respond in a direct and total way to this prophetic call: the religious orders who work on the streets, the doctors of *Medecins Sans Frontieres*. Yet not everyone can respond so directly. This is the humiliation of the comfortable; having understood that we are not the ones called to the extreme, we find excuses for doing nothing. So we need to ask our Lord to cast out that 'strong man fully armed' who guards our inner palace and makes sure our goods are undisturbed. Then we too, in our own way, can respond with crazy enthusiasm to the belief that the kingdom of God has overtaken us.

Thought for the day
He who is not with me is against me.

Prayer
Lord,
you say that if I do not gather with you then I scatter,
so I worry that I am at present scattering.
May the Kingdom of God so overtake me
that I become gathered into it myself
and so cease to scatter my energies elsewhere.
Help me to hear your voice clearly today.
Amen.

The only security

Hos 14:2—0; Ps 81, Mk 12:8–34

> *Israel, come back to Yahweh your God.*
>
> (Hosea 14:2)

Hosea is one of the most attractive prophets because he describes the intimate love that exists between the god called Yahweh and his partner, Israel. The Lord our God (Yahweh) invites Israel to turn away from her idolatry and her political alliances. Instead, she is to provide herself with words, specifically, with words of sorrow and love. Contrary to what people normally say, Hosea wants words not actions. Israel's actions have been the means by which she betrayed her Lord, connecting her to idols and to allies. By contrast, the words of love will come from her heart into the heart of God.

It would be all too easy to say that Hosea rules out politics as an expression of love, but that would be a very superficial reading. Hosea sees love as Jesus does: it is rooted in the personal love of God, the first commandment, and it expresses itself through love of neighbour. This love of neighbour can be expressed both in the literal, local neighbourhood, and in the national or international community. Just as in a local neighbourhood people pay protection money to a mafia gang in order to buy security, so too nations can make alliances to keep global bullies off their back. Hosea is saying that making alliances with Assyria, the superpower of his day, does not bring Israel security. Only faith in God can do that, 'because all your fruitfulness comes from me'.

More than ever today we live in a world of alliances. Nato, for example, is the most powerful military alliance history has ever seen. So how should we respond? By reminding ourselves that this alliance is not eternal and not infallible, so it does not merit our unquestioning faith. Some will reject it entirely on pacifist grounds, while others will award it a role. This role, however, is limited to the promotion of justice and the protection of the weak, not the selfish promotion of its member states' individual interests. Otherwise, alliances such as this cause sacrifices and holocausts to be offered to the false god of national self-interest. For Christians, loving our God involves the love of neighbour, which means every neighbour in the world.

Thought for the day
Read the media with discernment; in what you are being invited to place your trust?

Prayer
Lord,
help me to place all my trust in you.
Save me from the false gods that look so attractive on the
    surface
and keep me wisely devoted to you alone.
May I love you with all my heart,
all my strength
and all my understanding.
Amen.

Life-giving liturgy

Hos 5:15–6:6; Ps 51; Lk 18:9–14

> *Faithful love is what pleases me, not sacrifice;*
> *knowledge of God, not burnt offerings.*
>
> (Hosea 6:6)

Today's readings return to the Lenten theme of repentance and forgiveness. Performing religious rituals such as burnt offerings or fasting gets a bad press in both the reading from Hosea and in the Gospel reading. These sayings are grist to the mill of those modern sceptics who believe that the practice of religious ritual is hypocritical and pointless. In a previous era, when most British people were considered to be committed Christians, this charge was a poignant one. Today, however, Christian communities are often the most active in promoting repentance and justice. So, in an era of declining church attendance, we want to promote participation in religious ritual as a way of sustaining integrity and justice.

Somehow our religious practices must flow into loving lives and our loving lives must lead back to religious practices. The way we celebrate the liturgy can either be deadly in its disconnection from life or it can be life-giving in sustaining people who are living generously.

This is not simply about styles of worship: Mass celebrated casually does not mean it is connected to life, nor does a formal celebration with a choir mean it is disconnected. The quality of the celebration is what counts, not its style.

Quality in liturgy derives from several dimensions of life: from the community life that binds together those who comprise the assembly and from the prayerfulness of those who worship. Above all, it derives from the ability of the worshipping community to reach out to the surrounding community. In practice this means the ability to welcome visitors, to care for those in need and to initiate new members. In so far as we reach out to others from our worship then we enter the depths of the mystery of Jesus Christ whom we worship. In so far as we care for Christ's Body in our lives then we can sincerely celebrate the Body of Christ in the Eucharist. The care feeds the celebration and the celebration feeds the care.

Thought for the day
May we consider today how we will bring all the events of the week to the Lord in Mass tomorrow.

Prayer
Lord Jesus Christ,
we love the comfort of your Body at communion.
Help us to care for that same Body in the needs of family, friends and neighbours.
Give us a special care for the poorest both at home and abroad,
for your name's sake.
Amen.

Ursula Sharpe

Fourth week of Lent

Fourth Sunday of Lent

Blind spots

1 Sam 16:1, 6–7; 10–13; Ps 23; Eph 5:8–14; Jn 9:1–41

> *'Since you say, "We can see", your guilt remains.'*
>
> (John 9:41)

This week's readings include some inflammatory pieces. Jesus seems to be really pushing the Jews to react. He is 'right there in their faces' and is leaving them no option but to make a choice: 'Get rid of me, or follow me.' Even with his three miracles, he does all the healing on the day when it is forbidden to work. He even sounds irritated with the court official who asks him to come and heal his son: 'So – you will not believe unless you see signs and wonders?'

Jesus sounds tired; perhaps he is close to burn-out from his seemingly endless interactions with people. All they want to do is suck him dry of all he has; they do not seem to want to hear his message.

This Sunday we are looking at our blindness. The first reading tells us that God does not look at appearances but at what is in our hearts. It is often the most unlikely one who is the prophet and saint. For me, today's saints are the grandmothers living in the villages in Africa who are caring for their adult children as they die from AIDS. They are then left with ten or more orphans to try and care for, as there is no one else left alive and no social welfare to help.

In the second reading the 'blind' Pharisees meet Jesus, self-righteously asking him, 'We are not blind, surely?' Aren't we like them, thinking we are so aware, so concerned about our neighbours? And yet, in so many ways we are blind - and like to be so. If we were not, would the world be in the state it is in? Would we not speak out, take action when we see people being discriminated against, hungry, attempting suicide? In Ireland, for example, I have heard that up to one third of the adult population is on anti-depressants – is that not a cry for help?

Yes, we do pray for these poor souls, 'for the sick and the lonely and those who have no one to care for them', but are our prayers mere words without action? It might be a good discipline during these final weeks of Lent to read, and take seriously, James's letter and see what action he is inspiring in us. It might prove to be more of a penance than giving up alcohol, cigarettes or whatever it is that we are depriving ourselves of these days.

Thought for the day
What is my blind spot? Am I prepared to ask for help to see it?

Prayer
Dear Jesus,
Help me to want to see
those who need my help this week.
Help me to put action on my faith.
Amen.

Sent by God

Is 65:17–21; Ps 30; Jn 4:43–5

> *The royal official asked Jesus, 'Come down before my child dies.'*
>
> (John 4:49)

'Come down before my child dies.' How often have I heard the same request! Often it is, 'Come before my mother/father dies'. We have 4,000 people with AIDS in our Home Care Programme and unfortunately, unlike Jesus, we are unable to do 'distance healing'!

Anna had a husband and five children. They lived, like so many others, in a mud hut with a grass roof. Her husband was dying when I began to visit them. She was caring for him, for the children, and trying to keep the small banana plantation going, their only source of food. He died, and then Anna got ill. Her son Sekito, 10 years old, left school to care for his mother and four siblings.

One day I called to see them. Anna had a high fever, as had all five children as they cuddled around her on the floor of the tiny house. She also had a severe headache and was arching her head backwards and crying with the pain. The children all had fevers, mimicking their mother's (something I saw children do many times when their mother was very ill). I sat with them, gave whatever painkillers I had to Anna, and held and spoke to the children. Soon their fevers disappeared without any medication.

As I sat there Sekito told me he wanted to be a priest

when he grew up. 'Why?' I asked. 'God has been so good to us, sending you to care for Mama, that I want also to help Him.'

I felt the tears coming to my eyes, wondering how on earth he could think that God had been good to them.

Anna's condition deteriorated. One day when I called, I found her burial taking place. A neighbour took Maria, the 2-year-old, but as all their near-relatives were already dead from AIDS, the others – aged 10, 9, 7 and 5 years – were left on their own to fend for themselves. We helped to pay for their school fees, food and clothing and had our volunteer community worker keep an eye on them. They survived, like the thousands and thousands of others who are orphaned when their parents die from AIDS.

We can do all this thanks to CAFOD and their generous supporters. CAFOD funded the AIDS Home Care Programme from the mid-1980s, a time when it was very unfashionable to have anything to do with people with AIDS.

Thought for the day
When we give to CAFOD, do we know or care what our money is used for?

Prayer
Dear God,
Some of us will have many questions to ask you when we meet.
Until then, do not let us waver in our belief
that in all this suffering you are with us.
Amen.

Our pool of misery

Ez 47:1–9, 12; Ps 46; Jn 5:1–3, 5–16

> *When Jesus saw him lying there he said, 'Do you want to be well again?'*
>
> (John 5:6)

The healing at the Pool of Bethesda is today's Gospel story. Picture this crippled guy, let's call him George, who has been lying at the pool with several more people for 38 years. He had it made, as the people passing in and out to pray would throw him a few coins. He, and his long-time friends, would have known all the tricks of their trade as beggars.

Now here comes Jesus. 'Do you want to be well again?' he asks him. ('No way', thinks George, 'I have a nice easy comfortable life here, why would I want to change now?') So he whines … 'I have no-one to put me into the pool when the water is disturbed; and while I am still on the way, someone else gets there before me.' Well, he had got so used to telling everyone about how he was being victimised, that what else would he say?

Jesus was having none of his self-pity. 'Get up, pick up your sleeping mat and walk'.

There was no counselling session here. No expression of sympathy. No nods of the head and appropriate sounds and gestures. Simply, 'Get up and walk – and don't be leaving your mat behind to come back to!'

I always wonder what happened to him next, as he moved off on his new-found legs.

As for ourselves, we can get so used to sitting beside our pool of misery, gazing into it, and blaming others for what has happened to us, that we do not want to move. We do not really want to be cured, to let the feelings go, to change. That would take too much effort, and a new mind-set.

What is your 'pool of misery'? What does it look like? Who are the people sitting around it? What are you talking about? What changes do you have to make in your life if you are to get up and leave the pool-side behind?

Are you able to accept help?

Thought for the day
What in your life has it taken you 38 years to do?

Prayer
Dear Jesus,
I have got so used to my pool of misery
that I do not want to move away from it.
Help me this Lent,
to look for someone to help me to move on.
Amen.

The favourable time

Is 49:8–15; Ps 145; Jn 5:17–30

> *'At the time of my favour, I have answered you*
> *On the day of salvation I have helped you.'*
>
> (Isaiah 49:8)

This is a difficult line for us living in the economically developed world in the 21st century. We want everything *now* - and we give up on God if we do not get it. We think that now is the favourable time for whatever we want, but in many instances it is not so for God.

In Uganda, I was constantly asking God for help and being angry with him when he seemed not just deaf but cruel as well.

Paul was 8 years old. His parents had died from AIDS leaving him in the care of a 12-year-old brother, Robert. We found them in a small house, Paul lying on the floor, skin and bones and covered in vermin. He had a high fever, diarrhoea, and was paralysed from the waist down. Robert had dropped out of school to look after him – and he had no money for school fees anyway. He did some digging for a neighbour, who gave him food in return.

We took Paul to the hospital and Robert came to help take care of him. Days and weeks went by and Paul put on some weight and gradually improved, but still could not walk. We used to take him around the compound in a wheelchair and we grew very fond of him. Robert was better than any nurse or mother.

Then Paul's condition suddenly deteriorated and no medication seemed to work. One day I found Paul delirious, with a high fever and crying with the pain in his legs. He was lying on his side with his little arms outstretched and calling to his mother to take him. He could see her standing there beside his bed. I held him close but he still kept crying out to her. Eventually, he fell asleep, but when he awoke he was crying again, begging his mother to take him. I have never felt so upset, and I cried to God to please let him go and end his suffering, but God seemed deaf and Paul's suffering continued.

Eventually, Paul died and I carried his little body to the car, accompanied by Robert. His elderly grandfather took the body from me and we buried it shortly afterwards. But I was left with the question that I ask so, so many times in the midst of this AIDS pandemic: Why does God allow his little ones to suffer so much?, and Why, oh why was it not the 'favourable time' to answer my prayer?

Thought for the day
Why do little children have to suffer so much?

Prayer
Dear God
let the little children, especially the orphans,
know that you love them,
by sending people to care for them.
Amen.

The angry day

Ex 32:7-14; Ps 106; Jn 5:31-47

> *'I know you too well: you have no love of God in you.'*
> (John 5:42)

Today is the angry day of the week! God is angry with the Israelites, and Jesus with the Jews. As they say in Uganda, these are really 'strong' angers. We have to stand back from the force that we feel in the words, and not alone in the words, but in the threatened actions.

Poor Moses has to take the brunt of it, as God tells him in the first reading, 'Leave me now, my anger will blaze out against them and devour them.' Jesus tells his listeners, 'Besides, I know you too well; you have no love of God in you.'

Can I let those words sink into me and feel their explosion within? Am I shuddering at the force of them? Or do I think that God or Jesus would have no cause to be angry with me because I live such a good life? After all, I send money to CAFOD and to that wonderful nun on the missions, I pray for the hungry and the suffering in Sudan and elsewhere, and I always give a few bob to the Vincent de Paul. So the 'them' that God and Jesus are so angry with are other people, the rich, the greedy, the godless. But why not spend a few minutes letting the words sink into you and see if you still feel the same?

To continue the story, Moses now starts pleading with God, not to kill the people. Eventually, God relents. We see the same pattern with Jesus, eventually he too relents on the Cross, 'Father, forgive them for they know not what they do.'

I suppose that is the difference between God and me; between Jesus and me. Lots of people and events make me angry, and perhaps it is necessary at times to allow this anger to explode: at seeing the amount of money spent on alcohol while people dying of hunger, for instance. But what is the point of getting angry if I do nothing about it? After all, the only one that I can change is myself, and, as all change has a ripple effect on others, why not start changing now?

Thought for the day
Today, what might I feel justifiably angry about? What action will I take as a result?

Prayer
Dear God,
there are many things that I should give up,
and many things that I should take up.
Help me today,
to make one small change
that will be for the benefit of my neighbour.
Amen.

1,296 Hail Mary's

Wis 2:1, 12-22; Ps 34; Jn 7:1-2, 10, 25-30

As I write I am in Lough Derg, St Patrick's Purgatory, in Donegal, Ireland. It is a place of pilgrimage, where St Patrick is said to have done penance and where, for over a thousand years, people have come from all over Ireland and from many parts of the world to do likewise, through prayer and fasting for three days.

On arrival on the island one is divested of one's shoes. Each day one meal of dry toast and oatmeal biscuits is taken with black tea or coffee. No sleep is allowed the first night. I have been awake now for 36 hours and there are another 4 to go.

Prescribed prayers are said while the pilgrims go round the basilica, the six penitential beds (where, rumour has it, the stones are sharpened each night!) and other areas of this tiny space. The challenge is to avoid falling or stubbing your toes. Each 'station' takes at least one hour to complete.

I have said 792 Our Father's, 1,296 Hail Mary's and 240 Apostles' Creeds – and I still have another day to do! We have Masses, confessions, prayers galore. The night vigil is tough, with the stations inside the basilica. At times, we drag our bodies outside to try and stay awake only to be eaten by the midges or beaten by the freezing gales coming from the lake. It seems to rain all the time, and it is cold and miserable.

Yet, there are over 350 companion pilgrims here today, of all ages, and this is the pattern from June to August each year. Many return year after year. Why, you may ask?

Lough Derg is where you come face to face with your limitations. It is paradoxically relaxing, like a mindless mantra, where all you experience is this moment. For me, it is about being in solidarity with some of the suffering of our world: the numbed and hungry people of Darfur, Sudan, the cold of the Afghan refugees. It is raining constantly and I am wet, and I think of the people of Bangladesh trying to find a dry spot in the flood waters of their country. I experience the longing for sleep of the sleep-deprived victims of torture.

And then it is over, and we are on the boat back to the mainland. My fasting and suffering are over but as I thank God for all the little things that I have been taking for granted, I can pray in a new way, at least for a little while, for those who are so less fortunate than I.

Thought for the day
'Let us ... put his endurance to the test.'

Prayer
Dear God,
help us to give up something this Lent,
so that we may experience
a little of the misery of our many brothers and sisters.
Amen

On God's side

Jer 11:18–20; Ps 7; Jn 7:40–52

> *'I was like a trustful lamb being taken out to be killed,*
> *and I did not know what it was that they were*
> *planning against me.'*
>
> (Jeremiah 11:19)

An American friend of mine told me of her nephew who was a US army reservist, being called up to serve in Iraq. He was having his college fees paid by the army in return for being a reserve. He and his companion reserves were given two weeks of refresher training before leaving for duty, which included shooting. No wonder so many of those young men have been killed.

It reminded me of the very young soldiers we used to see in the north of Ireland. With their faces blackened, their fingers on the triggers, they would walk the streets looking around all the time. You could see the fear in their eyes and in their body movements.

These are the ones who fight our wars, who do the 'dirty work' for our politicians and for us, as our politicians have been voted in by us. They are like 'trustful lambs being led to the slaughter-house', when all most of them wanted was an education, lured to their death with the promise of school fees.

I often wonder what the world would be like if women were in charge of our defence forces. Would we be more concerned about sending our sons to be slaughtered? Would we be more compassionate towards the sons of the enemy? As we are the ones who give life, would we be less likely to take life as we remember the pangs of childbirth, and the joys and sorrows of raising these young men?

God must be having a hard time these days deciding who to listen to. There are Christians praying today's Psalm 7: 'O Lord my God I come to you for protection ... If I have wronged anyone ... let my enemies pursue and catch me ... let them cut me down and kill me ... justice is what you demand.' While there are Muslims praying to Allah with similar words, asking him to protect them and to destroy their enemies. Is that why the war in Iraq is taking such a terrible toll of lives ... ?

Thought for the day
Whose side do you think God is on?

Prayer
Dear God,
protect our young service men and women.
If they must die,
let it be quick,
but with time to know
that you are close by waiting for them.
Amen.

Patrick Lafon

Fifth week of Lent

Fifth Sunday of Lent

Living in hope

Ezk 37:12–14; Ps 130; Rom 8:8–11; Jn 11:1–45

> *'I am the resurrection.*
> *Anyone who believes in me*
> *Even though that person dies, will live.'*
>
> (John 11:25)

The prophet Ezekiel, deported to Babylon with the Jews in 587 BC, found signs of despair, desolation and death all around him. The Jewish people were demoralised. They had had their nation taken away from them and their temple in Jerusalem destroyed. Nebuchadnezzar of Babylon seemed all powerful; the kingdom he ruled over, invincible. Who would not give up in such dire circumstances?

Although Ezekiel talks about raising people from their graves, he is not referring to a physical resurrection but rather to the return of the deportees from Babylon. No matter how bleak the situation might look to human beings, he believed that God would liberate his people from the Babylonian yoke and return them in freedom to Israel.

Martha found herself in a similar kind of situation to the Jews. She had lost her brother Lazarus, and could not see any way out. 'Lord if you had been here my brother would not have died', she said. Yet she believed that nothing was impossible for Jesus: 'But even now I know that God will grant whatever you ask of him.'

Death and despair visit us in various and different ways: for example, in a relationship between a husband and wife that has gone sour because of infidelity; or a parish that has lost its way because of pride, rivalry and back-stabbing. While these may lead to a loss of hope on the part of individuals, sometimes situations arise that bring disaster and a feeling of impotence to entire nations. It is as if an entire people are held hostage. This is what happens when sit-tight dictators rig elections, loot the treasury, underdevelop their countries and remain in power for decades, terrorising all who dare question their right to rule.

Today's readings assure us that even in the most apparently hopeless situations, where from the purely human perspective there is no possibility of a cure, there is the possibility of transformation, thanks to God's action. The word 'despair' has no place in a Christian vocabulary.

Thought for the day
Death and decay cannot have the final say, because the spirit of God is in the world renewing all things.

Prayer
God our Father,
there are times of failure
betrayal, rejection, fear, discouragement
and even a loss of faith.
But we know that you are the Lord of time and history
and that evil will not triumph.
Amen.

Act with love

Dan 13:1–9, 15-17, 19–30; Ps 23; Jn 8:1–11

> *'The life of an innocent woman was spared that day.'*
> (Daniel 13:62)

Laura's story was all too familiar in the neighbourhood. This kind of thing had been happening with some frequency in the past years. Laura was about 17 and from a very poor family. After she had finished primary school, her parents couldn't afford the money to send her to secondary school. In any case. since she was a girl, and the education of girls was not seen as a priority, no one was overly worried that she was at home helping with the chores and farm work while her brothers were in school.

It was while all of this was going on that an acquaintance showed up and talked optimistically about sending Laura to Italy, where a lucrative job awaited her. Her parents were quickly won over and within weeks she received her passport and visa … to prostitution and slavery.

For seven years, Laura would be forced to do this 'work', while others kept the proceeds.

The experience of Susanna, daughter of Hilkiah and wife of Joakim, is a paradigm. It illustrates the particular vulnerability of women. 'Susanna' is the name of any woman who is forced to sell her body for money; who suffers female genital mutilation; who is prevented by law and by tradition from inheriting the property of her husband when the latter dies; who is threatened into becoming a wife to a man much older than her whom she neither knows nor loves; who is the first to be withdrawn from school when the money runs short; or who receives the death sentence for adultery without anyone bothering to remember that it takes two to tangle.

The list is long. It was thanks to the perspicacity and wisdom of Daniel that Susanna, who was looking death in the eye, had her life given back to her.

In today's Gospel, the story of the woman who had been caught committing adultery, Christ challenges the scribes and the Pharisees: 'If there is one of you who has not sinned, let him be the first to throw a stone at her.'

In other words, he asks us to act to save rather than to condemn; he was saying to us, 'Act with love'. What better attitude to adopt towards the Susannas of our time?

Thought for the day

There remained a great misery (*miseria*) and a great pity (*misericordia*). (St Augustine)

Prayer

Almighty and Eternal Father,
many people suffer innocently in our world today;
many women in particular are used, abused and even
    raped.
Give a new heart to women who suffer,
as well as to those who cause it.
Amen.

The right perspective

Num 21:4–9; Ps 102; Jn 8:21–30

> *'You are from below, I am from above;*
> *you are of this world, I am not of this world'*
>
> (John 8:23)

Who are the heroes that we most admire and desire to emulate? Who are the people who most inspire us and after whom we would like to model our lives? So often, they are glamorous film stars with thousands of dollars to spend, talented soccer players earning fabulous sums each week, or business tycoons with private jets.

God showed himself to the Israelites as Provider and Protector. He gave them manna and water in the desert. God was present in their most difficult moments. One might have thought that the people would trust him and rely on him for everything. Instead, they ran out of patience, and in their hunger grumbled about the 'unsatisfying food' that God was offering them. At one point on this journey to the holy land, they fashioned a golden calf, after the manner of their neighbours, and worshipped it.

St John Chrysostom tells us in one of his homilies that 'human beings are nailed to the things of this life'. How very true this can be in a world that glorifies material success of the very worst kind.

It would be wrong to condemn completely our quest for material well-being. After all, don't we have our families to feed? Don't we have the water and electricity bills to pay? Aren't there health problems that need medicines? What about the problem of poverty and underdevelopment in many Third World countries? And even in the affluent nations there are people sleeping rough. We certainly need material resources to address the problems of poor health care and lack of education and homelessness that threaten our humanity.

The problem is that we can become mired in materialism, making the mistake of thinking that what we have is more important than what we are. The good news is that when we allow our faith in God the Provider to inform our fight for material sufficiency and a more humane world, we acquire the right perspective with regard to the material goods entrusted to us.

Riches are useful - when they are shared and when they lead us from the below to the above.

Thought for the day
Are we caught up in the hedonistic philosophy of 'My Mercedes is bigger than yours'?

Prayer
Gracious God,
you are the giver of life and of every gift that we possess.
May we share your gifts to us with others
and receive your blessings in our lives.
Amen.

The courage to be a Christian

Dan 3:14–20, 24–28, 52–56; Jn 8:31–42

> *'It is better to obey God rather than men'*
>
> (Acts 5:29)

Lent is a time for naming the gods that we worship. It should be a time for shaming them as well.

In 1988 Tom Wolfe's *The Bonfire of the Vanities* was published. In this novel Wolfe identifies and holds up to ridicule some of the idols that our age offers incense to. Your imagination does not need to work overtime to identify what these gods are: money, success, sex, power and, I am tempted to add, sport.

Many people today betray a terrible weakness for the false gods that society erects for individual and collective worship. Some of us give in easily to people in positions of influence, in the hope of acquiring favours. Others simply run away from any situation that looks difficult, taking refuge in 'conventional wisdom'. Like King Nebuchadnezzar – who put pressure on Shadrach, Meshach and Abednego – the media, our peers and our superiors can sometimes put enormous pressure on us to conform to what is popular, rather than to what is right. Many of us give in, even if it means selling our souls to the devil.

On 3 September 2003 the Catholic Bishops' Conference of Cameroon published a Pastoral Letter on Corruption. In it they describe some situations when we have to make difficult choices:

'I want my child to become a student in a high school but the principal demands a bribe. If I don't give him money my child will be denied a place in the school. Will his future not be compromised?

'I may refuse to give the treasury official the 30 per cent of my salary he demands, but if he refuses to pay my salary how will my family survive ?'

The bishops conclude: 'Honest citizens have been known to say "No" to corruption, by refusing to pay bribes, which sometimes demands heroic courage.'

Shadrach, Meshach and Abednego had the faith and courage to stand up for the truth and against the orders of the king that everyone should worship the statue he had erected. In what was a life and death issue, they chose fidelity to God.

Thought for the day
'He who puts his hands to the plough and looks back is not worthy of the kingdom of God.' (Luke 9:62)

Prayer
God our Father,
We are sometimes afraid or ashamed of our Christian faith.
Give us the courage of our Christian convictions.
Amen.

Trust in God

Gen 17:3–9; Ps 105; Jn 8:51–59

> *'Your name shall be Abraham, for I will make you*
> *father of a multitude of nations.'*
>
> (Genesis 17:5)

One name that comes up repeatedly in the first reading and today's Gospel, that of Abraham, and in both readings Abraham is cast in a very favourable light.

God called Abram from Ur of the Chaldees and promised that he would make his descendants as numerous as the stars in the sky. But Abram and his wife were already well advanced in years and that could have legitimately sown some doubts in his mind. However, Abram trusted in God. In the first reading, God changes his name to Abraham. This change of name was not just a question of altering the way he was called: it is clear that he was giving Abraham a new identity and a new role in the history of salvation. God was entering a covenant with him because of his 'Yes'.

In Christian thinking, Abraham has become a model of what faith in God means. In his Letter to the Romans, Paul refers to him as our 'father in the faith' (4:16ff). He believed that the promises God had made to him would be fulfilled.

This is the opposite to the response of the Jews in today's gospel. Christ tells them the same unlikely things that God told to Abraham, but whereas Abraham believed and reaped the fruits of his faith, the Jews were enraged, and picked up stones to throw at Jesus.

Our age is reputed for its demand for scientific proof before it will give its assent. This is understandable to a certain extent, since ours is a scientific age in which every effect is thought to have a cause. Human beings, made in the image and likeness of God, are endowed with the intelligence to probe the causes of things, to use their reason to understand why things happen.

But life would become impossible if we didn't accept certain things on faith. For instance, a young child believes what her parents tell her, and accepts the choices they make for her, and rightly so. As she grows up, she learns how to use reason and experiment to make her own decisions, without losing her trust in the wisdom of her parents. Faith and reason are not in conflict with each other. Each has its legitimate place.

Thought for the day
Father, increase the little faith that I have.

Prayer
Lord Jesus,
in moments of trials, sustain my faith;
in times of difficulty help me to see your will;
in everything that I do, stay by me to give me the help I
    need.
Amen.

The gift of prophecy

Jer 20:10–13; Ps 18; Jn 10:31–42

> *'I have done many good works for you to see ... for which of these are you stoning me?'*
>
> (John 10:32)

The prophet Jeremiah was a native of Anatot, a town not far from the capital. He was a timid person whose greatest desire was to live a quiet life with his family. But unfortunately he lived in turbulent times. Although Israel had been almost completely overrun by Babylon, the king and the religious leaders were pretending that everything was going fine. When Jeremiah, acting on divine instructions, pointed to the folly of the religious and political elite, he became a target.

In the event, what saved Jeremiah from despair was the fact that God was by his side. The same was true of David, to whom Psalm 18 is attributed. It is a hymn in thanksgiving to God for freeing him from the threat represented by King Saul. All things considered, only God could have protected his life from such a menace, since Saul was powerful and had a whole army at his disposal.

The Gospel reading, the story of the Jews responding to Jesus' claims to be the Son of God by fetching stones with which stone him, follows the same pattern of opposition from those in power to a clear divine calling and the realisation that God is with his own.

It has never been easy to exercise the gift of prophecy.

Jeremiah was imprisoned and ended up in a muddy cistern for his efforts; it is sometimes no less difficult and risky today. It is often a very challenging experience for a Christian who wants to proclaim the word of God by word and deed. Sometimes one has to put up with the opposition of relations and friends. In some regimes, when the Church dares to point out how badly things are going, when it details the abuse of people's rights, when it calls for good governance, the reply is often to demand that the Church stay in the sacristy and stop meddling in politics.

That would certainly make for a safer and much more comfortable life. But, whatever the dangers, the world is better today thanks to the gift of prophecy in the Church. Having created us, called us and sent us out on a mission, God does not leave us at the mercy of those who oppose us.

Thought for the day
If the world is so decadent in spite of the missionary activity of the Church, imagine what it would be like *without* it.

Prayer
God our Father,
the world is in turmoil
but doesn't know whom to turn to for salvation;
may peoples and governments
accept and respect the Church's divine mission.
Amen.

The decisive battle

Ezk 37:21–28; Jer 31:10–13; Jn 11:45–56

> *'You cannot be a slave of God and of mammon.'*
> (Luke 16:13)

In this last week of Lent, and just before we enter Holy Week, the battle between Jesus and the religious authorities of his day gains in intensity. He had just raised Lazarus from the dead; this was alarming to many. What if the people should now want to make Jesus their king, thereby bringing the nation into conflict with Rome? The conclusion seemed inevitable: 'It is better for one man to die ... than for the whole nation to be destroyed.'

They were on the look-out for him. Given the animosity against him, was he going to turn up for the Feast of the Passover? While Jesus did not deliberately court confrontation, he was not going to walk away from his mission. He took some time off to consider his options, and then entered Jerusalem to face his adversaries ... and the Cross.

At this juncture, just before Easter, the battle against sin in our lives will be reaching a climax of its own, just like the struggle between Christ and the Jewish leaders. Unlike him, it sometimes seems that we can resist everything except temptation! Christ did not run away from this final confrontation with the forces of darkness but turned defeat into triumph through the Cross.

Make no mistake, this is the road we too are called upon to take. We will have to go to war against sin and all that keeps us attached to sin. If we will journey with Christ into Easter, now is time to win in a decisive way the battle we started against the devil and his false promises five weeks ago. There are no two ways about it: we must enter into decisive combat with sin. As the sacred writers say, he was not Yes and No at the same time.

In the vicissitudes of life, we should never forget that it is God's grace that helps us prevail. As we read in the first reading: 'The Lord says this: I shall cleanse them, they shall be my people' (Ezekiel 37:27).

Thought for the day
At baptism we make a clear commitment to be and remain God's children.

Prayer
Father,
on our pilgrim journey to your kingdom,
we often choose wrongly on account of human weakness.
Give us the grace of return,
and welcome us like the prodigal son.
Amen.

Jane Livesey
Holy Week and Easter Sunday

Passion Sunday

Preview day

Is 50:4–7; Ps 22; Ph 2:6–11; Lk 22:14–23:56

> '*I know I shall not be shamed …*'
>
> (Isaiah 50:7)

It is as though we are being given a preview – the week ahead encapsulated in today's liturgy. And what is our response? Probably, like the people who were there on that day, we want to airbrush out the hard bits, the painful bits, the bits that are going to make demands on us, as any following of this man – who is our God – inevitably does. We would like to stay at the festival, spreading our cloaks and our branches, shouting out our blessings on the healer, the itinerant preacher who has made such a name for himself and who might be the one to offer us an uncomplicated and easily won victory over our 'oppressors'.

But we are not given the opportunity to stay there in that comfortable and undemanding position of spectator. We are moved inexorably on to witnessing (which is very different from spectating, because it involves at least some degree of engagement) the start of the hard path that lies ahead of him, and of us, in this coming week. We are shown quite unequivocally the nature of Christ's kingship – that he does not and will not cling to his equality with God – and forced to face the mismatch between our hopes and expectations of his reign and what the reality will in fact be, for him and therefore for us. It will not be about who is the greatest, the richest, the most successful, the best protected from everyday realities but, instead, it will be about service, about humility, about reaching out to the wearied and about trusting that the Lord will come to our help even in the most appalling and despairing of situations for ourselves and for our world.

Our God is telling us, and showing us, that it will not be his power that saves us but his love.

During this week we are, once again, invited to enter into that mystery: to set our faces unflinchingly towards it, to wrestle with its paradoxes, struggle with its demands and, finally, rejoice in its overcoming of the darkness in the light of the Resurrection. Today we begin the final chapter …

Thought for the day

Mere waiting and looking on is not Christian behaviour. The Christian is called to sympathy and action; not in the first place by his own sufferings, but by the sufferings of his brethren, for whose sake Christ suffered.

(Dietrich Bonhoeffer, *Letters and Papers from Prison*)

Prayer

At the start of this most holy of all weeks,
we welcome you,
Christ our loving Messiah,
and we lay our lives before you,
that you may enter the gates of our hearts
and transform us into worthy members of your kingdom,
a kingdom of justice, love and peace. Amen.

A challenge to each of us

Is 42:1–7; Ps 27; Jn 12:1–11

> *'I, the Lord, have called you to serve the call of right ...'*
> (Isaiah 42:6)

For the first three days of this week we shall be presented with one of the most profound pen portraits ever written – that of Isaiah's 'suffering servant'. Today the concentration is on the servant's gentleness and on the very particular way in which he brings 'true justice to the nations'.

At the time of writing the United Kingdom's armed forces are still in Iraq – and there is little to indicate that they will not still be there by the time you read this. Whatever our views on the justification for the initial invasion and occupation we must at least acknowledge that this passage of scripture challenges it, and us, very radically – as do all the events of the forthcoming days.

The God who intervened in human history through his own Incarnation chose to do so in a way very different from the sort of interventions we have seen so many times in the past decade. He came - at birth, throughout his ministry and during his Passion and death - without 'crying or shouting aloud'. Even more importantly for all of us, he came without either wavering himself or breaking the 'crushed reed' that is each one of us at some point in our lives and, for many in large parts of the world, for most, if not all, of their lives.

In the same way, his entry into our human story also

challenges the ways in which the powerful nations of the earth have also chosen not to intervene in situations that appear to be at least equally desperate – and, more importantly, where the people put at risk by that decision not to act have been at least as much in need as those where intervention has taken place. Where to start? With the people of Rwanda, of the Congo, of Zimbabwe … and who knows which other peoples will be on that list by the time this is read.

The 'poor' are indeed always with us – and today we are challenged to question ourselves as to how, or even if, we play our part in bringing about the time when 'true justice is established on earth'.

Thought for the day

Lord, how liberal are you and how rich are they to whom you will grant your friendship.

(Mary Ward – Retreat notes, Liege, 1616)

Prayer

We pray you, God our loving father,
to give us the courage and the perseverance
to work faithfully to bring true justice
and, like your Son,
neither to waver nor be crushed by the weight of the task
but to continue to serve the cause of right.
Amen.

Why can't I follow you now?

Is 49:1–6; Ps 71; Jn 13:21–33, 36–38

> *'And all the while my cause was with the Lord, my reward with my God ...'*
>
> (Isaiah 49:4)

In today's gospel we read in the first line that Jesus himself was 'troubled in spirit'. It is very easy to miss that telling phrase - but we owe it to him to linger on it a little. Surely much of that being 'troubled' was the enormous loneliness that must already have been weighing upon him and which will increase exponentially over the course of the next few days as each of his disciples, in a smaller or greater way, finds that he does not have the strength, the fortitude, the courage just to stay there beside his Lord.

That human frailty – shared by each one of us – makes all the more striking Peter's rather outraged question at the end of the gospel passage, 'Why can't I follow you now?' It's a question we all ask in different ways at different times. Yet how often, when he does offer us the opportunity to follow him, do we say in one way or another, 'Oh, that wasn't exactly what I had in mind ...'. Choosing *which* Cross was not an option offered to Jesus and one of the painful lessons we have to learn is that, if we are truly to be his disciples, it is unlikely to be an option offered to us either.

It is more comfortable, and comforting, to focus on the Lord who is about to shoulder the burden of our redemption, as someone who is strong and able for the task and who commands our love and veneration for undertaking this on our behalf. But if he is also our brother and our friend (and if we are truly his followers, he should be both of those things) he deserves that we give time and attention to entering into the pain and loneliness of apprehension and anxiety and fear that must, by this stage of this week, have been crowding in on him and give thanks with our whole hearts that he was in it for 'the long haul' - whilst praying for the grace to be in it for the long haul ourselves too.

As always, Julian of Norwich has something simple but profound to contribute when contemplating both Our Lord, and ourselves as his disciples, at this point in the Passion.

Thought for the day

If there be anywhere on earth a lover of God who is always kept safe from falling, I know nothing of it for it was not shown me. But this was shown: that in falling and rising again we are always held close in one love.

(Julian of Norwich)

Prayer

We bring before you, O Lord,
all those in our world who seem to be toiling in vain
and whose lives are not accorded the dignity which they
    deserve.
May our solidarity with them, in word and deed,
give them hope and strength to believe that their cause is
    indeed with you.
Amen.

Who will listen … ?

Is 50:4–9; Ps 69; Mt 26:14–25

> *'For the Lord listens to the needy …'*
>
> (Psalm 69:33)

We live in a world in which the ability to listen is defined principally with reference to inanimate objects – the iPod, the CD, the DVD, listening through the internet on our desktops and laptops. As we walk down our streets or sit on the bus or on the train or on the Tube we see more and more people quite literally cut off from human intercourse, with earphones stuck in their ears, and a disregard for all that is going on around them – a disregard that ultimately leads to an alienation from our fellow human beings, to the point where we can just ignore them even when they are clearly at risk and in need of our help.

And yet, for each one of us, there is a need for our story to be listened to, to be heard and thus to be validated. And if so for us - the privileged, the 'haves' – then how much more so for our sisters and brothers who are 'needy' and 'in their chains' (Psalm 69:34)?

It must surely be part of our vocation, our calling (and the vocabulary is surely not coincidental) as followers of Christ to listen to the voice of the needy and to 'reply' to the wearied – and to 'reply' as Christ did, not just through what we say but through what we do.

How many others remember their mothers saying to them, as mine did to me, 'Well, Jane, actions speak louder than words'. And so indeed they do – but our actions, if they are to be authentically those of the Kingdom, must be based on a real understanding of what it is that requires our action and our 'zeal', and that understanding will not come through assuming that we know best and have all the answers. We must, rather, accord those on whose behalf we hope to act, the dignity of listening to their voice and then standing by them and with them in whatever ways are appropriate in order that 'God-seeking hearts' can indeed revive and 'the poor when they see it … be glad'.

Thought for the day
I never wonder at another's faults, I only wonder at God's mercy to me after so many failings.

(Mary Ward – Retreat Notes, Liege, 1618)

Prayer
We pray, O Lord,
for the grace to be receptive to your voice,
to listen like disciples as you wake us each morning to
  hear your word
and then to reply to the wearied,
not with our voices only,
but with our actions and our lives.
Amen.

Actions speak louder than words ...

Ex 12:1–8, 11–14; Ps 116; 1 Cor 11:23–26; Jn 13:1–15

> '*If I ... have washed your feet, then you should wash
> each other's feet ...* '
>
> (John 13:14)

With the advent of the Easter triduum we enter the period
of our salvation history when actions speak louder than
words to a degree never known before or since.

It is no theological or spiritual accident that the Church
juxtaposes the washing of the feet and the institution of
the Eucharist in this one liturgy. To what is our attention
being drawn? Surely to the fact that at the very moment
when he was about to return to his Father, Christ desired
to do everything he could to prepare and equip his disciples for the task ahead – the bringing about of his
Kingdom, of which they had little understanding.

As ever, it is Peter who bears witness to this lack of
understanding, in a way that makes him the disciple
with whom so many of us can most easily identify. Ever
the 'all or nothing' man, he moves from outrage (again!)
to wanting the whole washing 'package' – and we know,
as he as yet does not, that simply being washed from
head to toe is not sufficient to save us from our frailty
and weakness.

Peter is challenged – as always, with understanding,
with love and with compassion - by his Lord in that
beautiful action of having his feet washed. How does our
Lord challenge each one of us through this action, both in

our own lives and as Church? Does the reality we live match the rhetoric we preach?

It must also be no accident that both the events recounted and (as with all liturgy) re-lived today are shared experiences. It is clear from what Our Lord says in both accounts that he expects his followers to come together as community to celebrate and share the Eucharistic meal and to act together in service of his people and in solidarity with them. The bringing about of the Kingdom is a task that is shared by each one of us – as at the Last Supper, none of us are excluded and none are exempt. As we too gird our loins for the struggle that is upon us we can only ask for the grace to make his example of loving service characteristic of our lives as his disciples, both individually and as his Church.

Thought for the day
The Eucharist sets you on the way of Christ.
It takes you into his redeeming death
and gives you a share
in the most radical deliverance possible.

(H. van der Looy, *Rule for a New Brother*)

Prayer
On this day when we celebrate the start of the redemptive mystery,
when we raise the cup of salvation and ponder your example of loving service
we pray for the unity of all those who follow and serve you, Lord Jesus,
and for the coming of the day when the Eucharist,
the food for the journey of loving service,
will be the sign of what unites, rather than divides us.
Amen.

What is truth?

Is 52:13 –53:12; Ps 31; Heb 4:14–16, 5:7-9; Jn 18:1–19:42

> *'Though he had done no wrong, and there had been no*
> *perjury in his mouth ...*
>
> (Isaiah 53:9)

Not so long ago a former politician who had retired from the political fray in not altogether laudable circumstances was interviewed for television. The interviewer came to the conclusion that for the former politician, 'the truth was like a second home: he didn't live there all the time.'

Today is all about truth – Peter's denial of it; Pilate's incomprehension of it; the Jewish leaders' refusal to accept it; Christ's living of it, up to and including the moment when that demanded the handing over of his life; and John's witness to it 'so that you may believe as well'.

Jesus tells us, as he told Pilate, that it was to bear witness to the truth that he came into the world, and that if we are on the side of truth we will listen to his voice – and conversely, if we say we listen to his voice we must be on the side of truth. Being on the side of the truth is very often a lonely and uncomfortable place – but never more so than it was for Jesus.

Jesus also tells us that his Kingship is specifically related to being on the side of the truth and to bearing witness to that truth. If we are to be members of that Kingdom and to work towards its fulfilment we must take those words – and their demands - very seriously. It reminds us of that old question, 'If being a Christian were a criminal offence, would there be enough evidence to convict you?'

Today, of all days, as we gaze upon and walk alongside Jesus, the incarnation of Isaiah's suffering servant, bearing our sufferings and carrying our sorrows, we cannot run away from that hard-hitting question nor the truth of the answer which it elicits. And having faced that truth we must then go on to act in accordance with what we learn from it, demanding as that will be from time to time. On this day of all days we know that that is the least we can do ...

Thought for the day

That which is Christ-like within us shall be crucified. It shall suffer and be broken.

And that which is Christ-like within us shall rise up. It shall love and create.

(Michael Leunig, A Common Prayer)

Prayer

Lord Jesus,

as we gaze on you today,

bearing our sufferings and carrying our sorrows,

we pray most earnestly for our suffering world

and in particular for those parts of it where your people are planted in truly arid ground.

We pray too for ourselves

and for the courage and strength to play our part in the watering of that ground

so that your suffering servants can indeed prosper and be lifted up.

Amen.

Great expectations ...

Gen 1:1–2:2; Is 54:5-14; Mt 28:1–10

> *'On the seventh day God completed the work he had
> been doing ...'*
>
> (Genesis 2:2)

In Salley Vickers' novel *Miss Garnett's Angel* one of the
characters says, most memorably, that 'the greatest wis-
doms are not those which are written down but those
which are passed between human beings who understand one another'.

That kind of understanding was clearly present in the
scene between Jesus and the women at the end of today's
reading from Matthew. It was an understanding that was
the fruit not just of their years spent in his company
whilst he was going about his ministry but of their hours
spent standing at the foot of his Cross on the previous
day, in silent and weeping solidarity with him and with
his mother and the disciple whom he loved.

But that understanding was also the fruit of the time of
waiting that had come between, the whole of the Friday
evening and the whole of the Sabbath, respecting the
Law and adhering to it despite the temptation to do otherwise. That ability to sit with things, to be patient and
wait for the proper time is one that we have rather lost in
our fast food, fast everything culture, and with that loss
have come other losses – such as the loss of time devoted to relationships, the loss of a sense of connectedness
to our fragile but ever-rich environment, the loss of the

sense of mystery that is part of our human, let alone Christian, inheritance.

Some years ago, I spent some time in Australia. As a head teacher I had become aware of how entangled I had become in the 'hamster wheel' of life and I knew that God was giving me an opportunity to redress the balance. This happened in particular through my time among the Aboriginal people, who know all about Holy Saturday, in practice if not in theory, and whose culture has 'taught us to be still and to wait'. They talk of the gift of *Dadirri* which, among other things, sees the importance of waiting and taking time in order that 'things can be done with care' and 'in the proper way' because 'there is nothing more important than what we are attending to'.

There is indeed nothing more important than what today we are waiting for and attending to …

Thought for the day

We can do nothing, but God can do all.

(Mary Ward, Rome, 1625)

Prayer

God our loving Father,
on this day you invite us to wait and to learn the lessons of waiting –
our dependence on you,
our need of your grace and power
and our solidarity with those for whom hope is fragile and waiting is endless.
We pray for the grace to remain in this place,
to be patient and to trust in you
even in the face of seeming disappointment and disillusion. Amen.

'The glory of God is humanity fully alive'
(St Irenaeus)

Acts 10:34, 37–43; Ps 118; Col 3:1–4; Jn 20:1–9

You have been brought back to true life with Christ ...
(Colossians 3:1)

This is the day that the Lord has made, let us rejoice and be glad in it.

And so, at last, we have arrived at our destination – the journey is complete and we can rejoice unreservedly – or can we? Even now there is mystery and there is paradox. On this day of all days we are not presented with one of the resurrection appearances of Jesus – but with his absence from the tomb. And this time the disciples do 'get it' – there is not a moment's misunderstanding of what has happened. They know that he has risen – and so do we.

But even now there is a challenge for us as his followers. We cannot settle down, get comfortable, 'eat and drink in his presence', as long as his people all over the world continue to suffer, to be oppressed, to live without the dignity that is their human right. 'The glory of God is humanity fully alive': that is what the resurrection promises – and delivers. But as long as our world does not accord that dignity to each person in it then Christ's passion and resurrection have not finally fulfilled their purpose – and for that he needs us.

He needs our passion, our commitment, our generosity, our compassion, our 'zeal' for the coming of his Kingdom.

Like him, we cannot remain in the tomb but must press on in living out the consequences of the resurrection in our own lives and working and praying tirelessly that its consequences will become real in the lives of all his people. At the same time we need to retain the joy and lightness of heart that comes of remembering that we are not the Messiah, that God, through the death and resurrection of his Son, has already saved the world. All we are asked to do is to participate as fully as we are able in the work of salvation. The task, and the privilege, entrusted to us by our risen Lord today and every day is the same one entrusted to the late Archbishop Oscar Romero – to be 'prophets of a future not our own' and to remember that our work is 'a beginning, a step along the way, an opportunity for the [risen] Lord's grace to enter and do the rest.'

Thought for the day

Rise, heart, thy Lord is risen. Sing his praise
    Without delays,
Who takes thee by the hand, that thou likewise
    With him may'st rise …

(Easter – George Herbert)

Prayer

On this day when we have indeed been brought back to true life in you, Lord Jesus,

we give thanks that the stone which the builders rejected has become the corner stone

and that your Church can proclaim today and every day that

'We are an Easter people and Alleluia is our song'.

May we proclaim that message not with our voices only but in lives lived with joy and generosity.

Amen.

CAFOD is the Catholic Agency for Overseas Development. It is the official overseas development and relief agency of the Catholic Church in England and Wales. CAFOD has been fighting poverty in developing countries since 1962.

CAFOD believes that all human beings have a right to dignity and respect, and that the world's resources are a gift to be shared equally by all men and women, whatever their race, nationality or religion.

CAFOD is a member of the Caritas International Federation, a worldwide network of Catholic relief and development organisations.

CAFOD raises funds from the Catholic community in England and Wales, the UK government and the general public so that it can:

- promote long-term development, helping people in need to bring about change for themselves through development and relief work.
- respond to emergencies, providing immediate help for people affected by conflict or natural disasters.
- identify the causes of poverty and raise public awareness of them, encouraging supporters and the public to challenge the structures, policies and attitudes that reinforce inequality.
- speak out on behalf of poor communities, explaining the underlying causes of poverty and challenging governments and international bodies to adopt policies that promote equality and justice.

- promote human development and social justice in witness to Christian faith and gospel values.

Enacting Gospel values

CAFOD's work is one of the ways in which the Church expresses and enacts its belief in human dignity and social justice.

It is inspired by Scripture ('to bring good news to the poor,' Luke 4:18), by Catholic Social Teaching and by the experiences and hopes of the poor, marginalised and often oppressed communities it supports.

It works to enact Gospel values – within and beyond the Church – including:

- concern for our neighbours and the wellbeing of future generations
- serving the common good to enable everyone to develop equally
- fighting for social justice and ensuring everyone's basic needs are met
- acting on the basis of need, not greed, and acting in solidarity with those living in poverty
- promoting the values of human dignity, community, stewardship and the integrity of creation.

CAFOD puts into practice the solidarity and communion for which the Church stands, and strives for a world built on interdependence, mutuality and sharing, where exclusion, exploitation and greed do not exist.

Website: cafod.org.uk